THE LAST

F·I·V·E

MINUTES

THE LAST

F·I·V·E

MINUTES

The Successful
Closing Moves in
Sales, Business,
and Interviews

NORMAN KING

PRENTICE
HALL
PRESS

NEW YORK   LONDON   TORONTO   SYDNEY   TOKYO   SINGAPORE

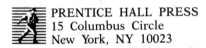PRENTICE HALL PRESS
15 Columbus Circle
New York, NY 10023

Library of Congress Cataloging-in-Publication Data

King, Norman
    The last five minutes : the successful closing moves in
sales, business and interviews / by Norman King.
        p. cm.
    Includes index.
    ISBN 0-13-524075-1
    1. Selling. I. Title. II. Title: Last 5 minutes.
HF5438.25.K563   1991
658.85—dc20   90-36089
                                                         CIP

Designed by Stanley S. Drate/Folio Graphics Co. Inc.

Manufactured in the United States of America

10 9 8 7 6 5 4 3 2 1

First Edition

To Barbara . . .
I Promise to kiss you more
. . . and argue less

CONTENTS

THE
LAST

·F·I·V·E·

MINUTES

1

The Importance of the End Game

The traffic on the George Washington Bridge was backed up for four miles and it took me an extra forty-five minutes to get to my apartment. I was exhausted and fed up. Besides that, I couldn't find a parking place on the street out front. When I finally did locate a spot two blocks away it began to rain. But that was all add-on misery.

The core of my discontent was entirely something else.

I had just blown the first truly big-time sale of my life.

I *had* him, damn it! I had him in the palm of my hand. And he just got up and walked away. Right at the crucial moment: the closing of the sale.

Oh, I was down, I tell you! Down and flat on my back. *On the mat*. Done in.

How had it happened? What had I done wrong? Worse, what had I *not* done right?

1

QUALIFICATION AND PREPARATION

All these thoughts whirled through my mind as I pressed the elevator button and started up to my room. I tried to sort out the questions first to answer them, but I was unable to concentrate on the point of the questions.

Months of intensive background work had gone into that sales pitch. I had done an in-depth study of my prospect's background—all according to Hoyle. I had analyzed his company's needs. I had made up a chart qualifying *his* needs. I knew the product inside out: it was a complicated machine, used in a very special procedure my client needed in his department.

He needed it. *I* needed it. The *price* was right. I wanted him to sign on the dotted line. But . . .

WHEN EVERYTHING BEGAN TO FALL APART

The turning point had been reached after a half hour's very amiable talk early that afternoon. I was simply waiting for the strategic moment to sink in the hook.

"Can you deliver after ten days' notice?" he asked me, almost as if he had anticipated my move, which was to lead him into asking me when we could make delivery.

Bingo! I said to myself. I was elated. "No problem," I said casually, and smiled at him. It was all over. I had my fish hooked! Now it was only a matter. . . .

He stood up and shook my hand. "Good. I'll be in touch." He was leading me by the hand to the door—forcing me across the space with his elbow and shoulder actually— and at the door he patted me affectionately on the back. "Real nice talking to you."

I guess my mouth was hanging open so far you could see all my dental work—even the root canal.

It was over. I had let him slip off the hook. *How* had he done it? He *wanted* the product. He wanted to do business with me. He was ready, willing, and able. How had I let him go?

Shaking my head, I opened the apartment door now and turned on the lights. The rain was beating on the window outside, but it was stuffy and hot in the apartment. I tore off my tie and stared at myself in the mirror. With loathing.

"Jerk! Stupid! Loser!"

THE STORY OF JEFF THE MAGNIFICENT

Even a splash of cold water in the face was insufficient to revive my sunken spirits. I changed into my slacks and T-shirt and wandered into the study where I kept my papers and did my homework. On the way I passed the little table in the short hall connecting kitchen and bedroom. The chess board was set up as always and the latest postcard was propped up against the wall.

Good old Jeff! I thought with a half-smile. Now *he'd* never allow himself to louse up a sale the way I had. He was a winner—always had been. We had grown up together in the old neighborhood and were of an age. It was he who introduced me to chess when we were in high school.

After college he had gone into the diplomatic service, had struck it rich in his very first assignment, and was now one of those free spirits the government sends here and there as troubleshooters and fix-it men for the State Department. Lucky Jeff! No. *Skillful* Jeff. *Brilliant* Jeff. *Successful* Jeff.

CHESS BY POST

Because we could no longer sit down as neighbors to a delightful chess game in the twilight hours of the day, we were forced to play one of those chess-by-mail tournaments—ongoing always, but strung out for weeks and months before completion. A move. A postcard to him. A postcard from him. His move. My move. A postcard to him. And so on.

I stared down at the board. His latest move was on the postcard propped up behind it. We were in the end game now—the most important part of the contest. And he had me in a bind. A really bad bind. I had sat there all the night before, trying to figure out how to avoid the trap he had set for me.

We were down to seven pieces, and of course Jeff was one up on me. But now it wasn't the number of pieces, or even their strengths: it was a matter of *position*. I had just a slight advantage there. But he was steadily and remorselessly applying the pincers to me. Unless I could see what he was really planting and move against it. . . .

SAUL ON THE ROAD TO DAMASCUS

Suddenly, as I stared at the chess pieces on the board, thinking vaguely of Jeff out there in the Near East, trying to use diplomatic magic on the Syrians—of all people!—I had a sudden insight, quite like the binding flash that shattered Saul on the Road to Damascus and transformed him into Paul, the Disciple of Jesus Christ.

You see, suddenly *he* was not Jeff at all, and *I* was not me. I was Jeff, and the person standing looking down at the board was my client this afternoon. And *he* was thinking exactly what I had been thinking. He was looking at the trap that was forming for him, and he was trying to see his way around his opponent—me!

And, you see, I realized that he had very deftly anticipated my closing move. That would have been a question from me along these lines:

"When do you want delivery on the machine?"

THE WAY OF THE WINNER

Had I been able to deliver that line, my prospect would most probably have fumbled and hemmed and hawed, but eventually would have come up with a date. And the sale would have been consummated.

Instead, he had anticipated my closing move, and had forestalled it by asking me a question before I could ask *him* the crucial, closing question. As I stood there, excoriating myself for my idiocy, it came to me. Blinding flash of light, and all. *This* is what I should have said, reacting to his ploy that had cut me off at the pass:

HE: Can you deliver after ten days' notice?
ME: Shall I have it sent to the main office or to the branch we were talking about?

Then he would have paused, thought, and finally told me where to send it. I had blown it by not asking a question in response to *his* question. By throwing away the advantage by my fatuous, overconfident riposte—"No problem!"—I had lost the sale! It would take weeks to get at him again. Weeks!

I had forgotten the golden rule.

> *Golden Rule:* The question in response to the question is the barb in the hook. Once you have your quarry on the hook, the barb holds it inside his mouth. Otherwise . . .

THE PROPER MOVE TO CHECKMATE

Now I was studying the chessboard with renewed concentration and with a new-found vigor. I had pulled a blooper, but I knew now how I could avoid doing it ever again. At least that was *something*. Next time, next time, next time. . . .

And as I stood there I saw what Jeff was trying to pull. He was, in effect, trying to sink in the hook in exactly the same way that I had been trying. And he was just a little bit overconfident, the way I had been.

For example, seven moves ahead I could use my rook to block off Jeff's queen, and by bringing up my king, I could. . . .

I made my move, jotted it down on a postcard, added a special "thank you" to him—he'd never be able to figure out what *that* meant—and I was soon munching away at my frozen chicken dinner. It didn't taste at all bad tonight. At least now that I had begun to use my brains again.

My thoughts strayed to chess and business.

CHESS AS A BUSINESS GAMBIT

It was obvious that chess and business were parallels. For example, you could divide up any good sequence of salesmanship moves into the three main parts of a chess game: the opening gambit, the middle game, and the end game. Just like a three-act play.

Interestingly enough, I could see clearly that the opening gambit—usually called simply the *opening game*—was exactly what I did when I was performing the usual rites on a prospect:

- Preliminary research on prospect and company
- Qualification of prospect for product
- Analysis of product in terms of benefits for prospect
- First one-on-one contact with prospect after completion of preliminary preparations
- Establishment of specific goal for the call

THE GIVE-AND-TAKE OF THE MIDDLE GAME

Immediately my mind moved on to the middle game, and I could see the parallel there, as well:

- The first five minutes of the initial interview (Of course I'd already written a *book* about that, hadn't I?)
- Exploration of the prospect's needs, gleaned from my preliminary investigations, but now brought to the surface to study in words

- The give-and-take as each of us sounds out the other
- My own introduction of the product or service in a brief and punchy one-on-one presentation
- The give-and-take regarding objections and drawbacks
- The final analysis of the product's benefits

THE VALUE OF THE END GAME

And then the end game—the most important part of all. Look how important it had been to me, just tonight! Yes. There were the same moves:

- Circling around one another
- The psychological moment to sink in the hook, i.e., start the closing
- Pulling the hook in tight without letting it slip
- The final closing

Just like that!

It gave me an idea. By studying a little about the nuances of chess and analyzing what its masters had thought about it through the ages, I might very well discover something new for my own good—say, chess elements that might make me a better salesman. Why not? Transference was very big in psychology; why not in business?

I got a pile of books out of the library and began my research, and discovered to my delight that my instincts had been absolutely right! A sales program was almost exactly like a chess game; that is, the step-by-step preparation for and execution of the game (from opening gambit through middle game to end game) paralleled a chess match to a T. A good businessman could learn a great deal from chess, just as a chess player could learn a good deal from a study of business tactics.

A GAME FROM THE EAST

No one *really* knows where the game of chess originated, but it has been with us since before the birth of Christ, known principally as the most cosmopolitan game in recorded history. Invented somewhere in the East, its birthplace has variously been pinpointed in Greece, Italy, Babylon, Scythia (now part of the USSR), Israel, Persia (now Iran), China, India, Spain, and even Ireland and Wales. And from there—wherever it was—it has spread to every part of the civilized world.

It is played not only as a mere pastime, but as a serious game that has obsessed some of the finest minds in the world. A true chess master must spend his life to obtain even a fair understanding of the game, and chess abounds in so many subtle variations that it can be used to sharpen any professional's competitive edge and call forth pools of brilliance the player may never have known he or she possessed.

To me, the opponents in a good chess match can easily be equated to two generals deploying opposing troops on a battlefield; the strategies and tactics are eerily similar in spirit and in intent.

RUY LOPEZ, EVANS, THE SICILIAN, AND SO ON

Without going into the nuances of the various moves—there are at least six different pieces, each with different moves and strengths and weaknesses—suffice it to say that the game is divided into three separate parts: the opening game, the middle game, and the end game.

Because openings are so important, chess openings have been analyzed at length through the ages, with the best of them set out in books for a serious player to memorize. These openings have fancy names like the Ruy Lopez, the Sicilian Defense, the Evans Gambit, the English Opening, and so on.

The middle game in chess is a separate entity in itself. Using the positions established in the conventional opening game, each opponent is on his or her own in the middle game, and it is up to the individual then to evolve plans and prepare combinations that will lead to success. It is here that the individual's ingenuity must exert itself; it is talent, foresight, imagination, and sudden insight that brings the game to its final phase. But without playing a skillful middle game, the player cannot hope to begin the end game in a position to win.

THE SPECIALTY OF THE HOUSE

Which brings us to the end game. This is a special study in itself. In the end game the ordinary values and strengths of the pieces shift dramatically. Certain advantages and disadvantages suddenly exchange places. In fact, the value of each piece undergoes a sometimes radical change. The king, which is weak in the opening game and in the middle game, can become an active force of destruction in the end game. The pawns, which are negligible factors in the opening game and even in the middle game, now may become as strong as the queen, the overall power piece in chess. The knights and bishops lose strength, as do the rooks.

Even to someone who has never played chess, it is obvious that the opening game and the middle game are crucial to the success of the end game. But at the same time, while a player may start the end game with a decided advantage, all that combined strength and position may be dissipated before the final act of the end game and checkmate (or draw).

For this reason I feel that the final five minutes of any interview—for a business transaction, for a sale, for a job—is as important as the end game in chess. Yet, of course, as in chess, without the rest of the game (of business), and without the years of practice (at business) the player must take to master the game, the last five minutes—like the end game in chess—will be meaningless.

THE DUEL IN BUSINESS

Business is a game quite like chess in its applications; the opposite is true, also. Business is unlike war in that both sides come out winners; or, at least, one side is *not* a loser. But the duel between the two players in a business transaction certainly parallels the duel between two chess players; the same is true of two businessmen working out a complex transaction, and of a prospective employee and an employer.

In business we do not play with complex moves like the knight's: two forward and one to the side, or two sideways and one forward or backward, or two backward and one to the side; nor do we have to remember that the rook moves laterally and up and down; nor that the bishop moves diagonally; nor that a pawn's first move can be one square or two—and so on and so forth.

In business we are dealing with products, with services, and with people. The product may be small, large, or of many shapes and sizes. The service may be almost anything imaginable. The people are infinitely variable.

PEOPLE, ONE-ON-ONE

Instead of pieces on a board, in business one deals with people one-on-one. Instead of dice to toss or pieces to move, we deal with the wits and imaginations of each, and depend on the interplay between our personalities for the outcome of whatever negotiations we are conducting.

Like the end game in chess, the last five minutes can be equated to the final countdown of a space probe. From five minutes we count down from fifty-nine seconds to one, then from four minutes down to one second, and so on. If you've prepared your opening game right, and played your middle game with precision and care, then by the time for countdown, you'll be able to make the end game work to your advantage.

OUT OF SIGHT OF THE PROSPECT

Jack Falvey recently wrote that the most important step in any sale takes place without the presence of the customer or the client.

He meant that the preparation for the closing minutes of a sale was of primary importance. He meant that the development of the proposal, the long discussions held with the client, the contract negotiations, everything right up to the moment the final signature was affixed to the contract was of primary importance.

Each step was a part of a sequence of moves similar to those on a chessboard.

The culmination of it all was the final moment of the wrapping up of the contract.

PROSPECT: Can you deliver after ten days' notice?
YOU: Shall I have it sent to the main office or to the branch we were talking about?

Gotcha!

2

Preparation for the Successful Closing: I. Know Your Product

KNOWING ALL THE ANSWERS

The average salesperson *must* know the product or the service he or she is selling *inside out*.

> PROSPECT: What's the horsepower of Model G?
>
> YOU: Twelve and one-eighth horses.
>
> PROSPECT: How long is it?
>
> YOU: Eight feet three inches.
>
> PROSPECT: Will it perform over an hour without heating?
>
> YOU: Absolutely. It's guaranteed to work for one hour and forty-five minutes.

PROSPECT: Weight?
YOU: Three tons twelve hundred pounds.

And that's how you sell products—by knowing all about them from inside out. You can't be ignorant and say, "I don't know." You *must* know. Knowing the product is the very first move in selling the product.

HE KNEW THE PRODUCT

We'll call him Frank. Frank was handling air conditioners at the time he called on a friend of mine. My friend was running a small publishing company on the East Side in a rundown building that was on its last legs.

Frank entered my friend's office in his usual amiable fashion, and began to exchange a few witticisms to break the ice, when he realized that he was perspiring and almost gasping for breath after five minutes in the place. In short, there was no ice to break in that hotbox.

In the window of the office an air conditioner was wheezing and blowing as if it were in cardiac arrest. Frank glanced at it and walked over to the ailing piece of machinery, at which he stared long and hard.

"This thing is dying, friend."

"I know," groaned the publisher. "That's why I called you. Norman said you'd recommend a good one for me."

FRANK'S MAGIC ACT

Frank had removed the cover by then and was toying with the mechanism inside. Suddenly the wheezing stopped, and almost magically the machine began to hum and purr the way it was supposed to do.

"What did you do?" my friend cried in astonishment.

Frank shrugged ruefully. "What else? I just lost myself a sale."

Perhaps so. But by tinkering with the innards of the machine and straightening a bent part Frank had gained something else more important—he had modeled himself into an image of integrity and honesty.

"I was tempted," Frank admitted to me later. "It was a simple adjustment. But I couldn't let the poor guy purchase a new unit, especially when that building of his was condemned and he was going to have to move the firm anyway."

My friend's new offices were in a bigger building uptown, and when he made the move six months later, he let Frank provide air conditioning for the entire suite of offices—two whole floors of a marvelously modern building!

And all because Frank knew the product he was selling—better, probably, than some repairmen might have known it. I guess there's a moral here somewhere, but basically, it's the same old story. Know your product as you know yourself. By knowing it, you can usually make it work for you to earn good sales commissions.

TO TALK OR NOT TO TALK

There are a lot of quaint stories about Vermonters and their taciturnity. For example, a city man drives into a small village in Vermont. He's looking for Pomfort, but there are no signs at all in this collection of stores and houses. He alights from his car and strolls into a small dry-goods store where he confronts the proprietor.

"Can you tell me how to get to Pomfort?" he asks.

The proprietor looks up, studies the traveler, licks his lips, and says simply: "Don't move a derned inch."

This story isn't so much about a Vermonter's taciturnity as it is about the state's aversion to putting up road signs announcing villages and towns. If you ask a Vermonter why there are no signs, he or she will shrug and say: "Everybody *knows* it's Pomfort."

Yes. Everybody in Pomfort certainly knows, and everybody in the towns around that mythical place knows, too. But an outsider doesn't know. The outsider only sees a collection of neat little houses and well-kept farmland around the small two-block village.

The unmarked Pomfort has the same problem an unknown product has to someone viewing it for the first time. It takes someone else other than the person who made the product to point out its benefits and its advantages. Without someone to *feature* them, the product just sits there, hiding its beauty like an overmodest maiden.

DOES ANY PRODUCT "SELL ITSELF"?

I'm reminded of a recent well-circulated television commercial to the effect that a certain product *sells itself*, yet for the life of me, I cannot *remember* what product it is—proving the effectiveness of *that* sales pitch! The truth is, no product sells itself; every salesperson worth his or her salt *knows* there is no such product.

Without someone to talk about it, to extol its merits, to show how it can make life easier for the buyer, usually the product simply sits on the shelf or in the bin, and, like the stranger looking for Pomfort, doesn't "move a derned inch."

Note: The word "product" tends to be an all-inclusive word that is used quite freely—sometimes too freely—in conversations among salespersons. For the moment, let's look at what a *product* can be. It can be tangible: a piece of merchandise, a commodity of some kind, a manufactured thing, or a piece of equipment. It can be intangible: a service, perhaps, or an invisible aid of some kind. No matter what the shape, size, or consistency of the product, it will have a built-in utility or value to the buyer. In other words, it will do the buyer some good simply by belonging to him. This attribute is separate, but not inseparable, from the product itself. In the field of selling, it is absolutely essential for the salesperson to tap this resource of the product to stimulate the buyer to possess it.

Thus selling any kind of product generally involves a sales technique that causes it to move from seller to customer. That is stating the case baldly and without particular nuances in sales methodology. These techniques include illuminating the best sales features of the product, knowledge of the competition, an understanding of the sales prospect's needs and desires, and so on.

Interestingly enough, as we'll find out later on in this book, the strategies and tactics used to sell a simple thing like a vacuum cleaner also suffice to sell a multimillion-dollar company, or to put together a conglomerate of complex proportions.

> *The point is:* You'll be reading often in this book about the "product." Please be aware that it can describe anything from a box of matches to a conglomerate worth billions of dollars.

THE FAB FORMULA

Every product on the market has its own individual differences, its own variations from the norm. Each variation from the norm has been built into the product for a specific reason. You must be able to tell the prospect the reason *why* such a variation has been utilized.

Most salespersons know exactly what is involved here, whether or not they call these nuances by the FAB Formula or not.

For us now, the key word is FAB.

"F" Is for Feature

The features of a product are obvious: They are the actions or accomplishments the person who owns the product can expect from it.

- A man with a copier uses it to copy a letter he has just written.
- A man with a copier uses it to copy the page of a book he finds worthwhile.
- A man with a copier uses it to duplicate a photograph or a newspaper clipping he needs.

The ordinary copier usually has other added features as well as the simple ability to copy. Many copiers enlarge and diminish pages so that you can reduce the size of a tabloid-size newspaper to a regular typing sheet; and perhaps you can blow up tiny type that is virtually unreadable into a clear and visible text.

Another copier may have the capacity to copy in colored ink. Still another may have a changeable cassette to cut down on maintenance costs.

Note that the "features" described here are the kinds of tasks the copier can perform.

No salesperson is worth the powder to blow him up if he cannot recognize, understand, and extol lucidly the basic features of the product he or she is selling.

The magic word is still FAB. Let's move on to "A."

"A" Is for Advantage

A product's feature that duplicates a similar feature in the competition is simply a feature and nothing more.

But:

A feature that does something that no other copier does is a feature that has a definite *advantage*.

Advantage makes Copier A better than Copier B. However, the advantage must be noted and introduced by the salesperson so the prospect knows what it is.

Say, for example, that Copier B has a reducing feature that Copier A does not have. You will immediately think that Copier B has a *distinct advantage* over Copier A.

But this is not necessarily so. Suppose the prospect for Copier A does not want a reduction mode in a machine. For him Copier B has no advantage over Copier A. In fact, because Copier A may have a superior feeding mechanism, Copier A has, for him, an advantage over Copier B.

Advantage is a complex and versatile factor in salesmanship. It adds to—or subtracts from—the desirability of Product A over Product B.

Advantage is a word that has a built-in antonym, a word that means exactly the opposite: *disadvantage.* Thus a product's feature can be a double-edged sword. It can cut for one customer, but can cut back for another. It is the responsibility of the seller to channel advantages in the proper *direction* for the prospect.

Let's look at the key word again: FAB. Now let's try "B."

"B" Is for Benefit

It is now obvious that a product's advantage may not be an advantage for everyone who wants to use the product. The salesperson must realize that in order to sell a product, he or she must adjust the advantages and disadvantages a particular product may have for a particular potential customer—and organize and format them as *benefits*—so that the potential buyer will know how the product can serve him or her to maximum advantage.

There is a simple mental trick you can use to translate a product's advantage to a benefit for the buyer: simply explain exactly what the use of the advantage will mean to the possessor of the product.

I just purchased a cordless phone for myself. It's one of those handsets you plug into your regular phone, extend an antenna, and take the handset with you wherever you are in or around the house.

Having a handset is an advantage of sorts, but actually for someone who has a one-room apartment with the telephone handy at all times there is no advantage to a cordless handset at all. In my case, I am frequently out in the garage or in the yard puttering around over the weekend. For me the benefit is obvious. I am much more mobile than I used to be when I would step outside and keep listening long-distance for the phone that might ring.

No one had to tell me about this advantage; I understood it. If I had been called upon to sell such a product, I would have been able to imagine a number of reasons for having a cordless phone. As a salesperson, you have to consider the customer as someone who may not have really thought about the benefit of the product you are showing.

I could have toted up these benefits myself:

1. Carrying the cordless handset into another room of the house while conversing
2. Hunting for some piece of illusive information in nooks and crannies with the phone in hand
3. Taking the phone into a remote and closed room during a party for a private conversation
4. Putting the cordless phone in the bathroom while you're taking a shower or bathing, thereby obviating the rush through the house without any clothes on

And so on.

USING THE FAB FORMULA

The trick of using the FAB Formula to its maximum advantage is in developing your *imagination*. Imagination is sometimes considered a dirty word in our society; imagination can be equated with daydreaming, with wasting your time thinking of other things, with letting your mind drift, and with losing your concentration on the more important things in life.

However, there is a great deal to be said for harnessing your imagination and using it to think of new activities for a product to indulge in. Instead of letting your mind wander into pleasant pastures of golf and yachts and lolling on the beach at Tahiti, next time you are driving on a crowded highway, put your mind to your product and think of new ways to use it.

You'll increase the number of benefits and at the same time increase the number of sales you'll make with your next interview.

KNOWING ABOUT YOUR PRODUCT

One of the first jobs when you become assigned to a new product, or when you are hired to sell it, is to find out all you can about it right away. Except for some very simple article—a hammer or saw, for example—most products today are complex amalgamations of machinery and electronic wizardry. The more complicated the product, the more difficult it may be to understand it.

It is not a bad idea to talk with people who have designed a product in the first place, who brought it along in its developmental stages. I refer to the engineers who worked on it in its formative stages and saw the finished product as the tiny pinpoint of light at the end of a long dark tunnel.

In most cases this may be an impractical thing to do, since the product may have been engineered and built in Korea or even farther away. If these people are available for consultation, you should do everything possible to talk to them about the product in question.

Such discussion may give you new insight into an understanding of the particular aims of the product; you may also find out important details about how it works. Once you understand these elements, you can probably think of a number of new uses to which it can be put.

Actually, the practical *use* of a product may be quite different from the *intent* of its developers. Never blind yourself to wildly imaginative possibilities for it, even if the engineers may not have thought about what you want to use it for.

If it works—don't knock it.

Sources of Product Knowledge

In addition to what engineers have to say about a product—provided you are lucky enough to contact them—you should definitely involve yourself in discussions with customers who have used it and are familiar with it. In many cases you will find that their practical knowledge of product uses are much more cogent and important to you than what the engineers think of it.

Owners of products like cars are easy enough to locate for an approach. So are owners of smaller products like washing machines or vacuum cleaners. You probably won't have to move out of your neighborhood to find them. The same is true of such modern conveniences as personal computers and telephone-answering machines.

When you get into complicated machinery like printing presses or specific machines built for factory work, you'll simply have to visit plants that use your main competitor's machinery.

As you can see, a little detective work won't ever hurt you in trying to ascertain the real worth of a product as seen through the eyes of an owner and user.

Look Those Limitations in the Eye

You should also get some idea of the *limitations* your own product has. Knowing them is just as important as knowing its good working features. In business, it is a definite "no-no" to ignore limitations—worse, to pretend that they do not exist. You must make yourself aware of the bad features of a product as well as its good features in order to discuss it honestly.

Never forget: Honesty is not the best policy. Honesty is the *only* policy in salesmanship!

Principal Sources of Information

Usually you can rely to a certain degree on the promotional literature that is published about a product: the maintenance and usage manuals, bulletins, and samples.

Nevertheless, it is important to realize that a lot of sales literature is long on hard-sell material, exaggerated claims, and optimistic descriptions of performance. Also, as you read it, you will realize that most of it does not really do what you are going to have to do for yourself: explain to the prospective customer what the product can do for him or for her.

The point is, these principal sources of information about the product are all right as backups for your own sales presentations, but they should never be used without a great deal of your own input. Otherwise you will find most of your customers totally turned off by the literature, or turned on in an unrealistic and exaggerated fashion—expecting more than they will ever get. Neither extreme is permissible.

PUTTING TOGETHER A PRODUCT PROFILE

It's a good idea for you to get down on paper all the facts that I have discussed up to now. You may not always be selling Product A; you may in fact have a half dozen products you're pushing at the same time. For each product, you should make up a *profile*. A product profile is exactly the same thing as a personality profile: it contains all the features of a product, the characteristics of a product, and its advantages and benefits.

Using the FAB Formula, you can easily build up a quick inventory of the product, labeling its features, advantages (and disadvantages), and benefits on a sheet of paper or on a three-by-five file card.

At the top of the page, name the product.

Then, in three vertical columns, list product features in column 1, product advantages in column 2, and customer benefits in column 3. For each feature, put down the feature's advantage (or advantages), and its benefit (or benefits).

Soon you will be able to make use of your product library, flipping to the right card or page for a quick run-down of the particular product you need reference to.

You may find that you will need a product profile for each model of the particular product you are selling. In that case, specify the model in the product title. Be sure to keep the file up to date, noting all changes in the product, and filing information on new add-ons that are featured by the company.

WHAT TO DO ABOUT COMPETITION

The life of a salesperson is an uneasy one. Not only must the salesperson arouse in the customer a need for and desire to possess the product, but he or she must also recognize and combat competitive products that are being marketed to the same prospect.

Henry David Thoreau made literary history when he remarked in an off-the-cuff speech one night:

The world will beat its way to the door of a man who makes a better mousetrap.

He was teasing. He knew that no product itself attracts attention. It is the salesperson who does that.

It is selling that brings people in droves to the door of the man with the better mousetrap. Your main hope is that your product is actually *better* than all others.

Yet it is a solid statistical fact that of a hundred competitive products, only *one* is superior to all the other ninety-nine. However, by juggling features, advantages, disadvantages, and benefits to the customer, you may be able to make your product more viable and *practical* for the prospect you have in mind.

You must keep the idea of competition in mind at all times. You must know exactly how your product compares to the competition. You must know in what areas your product fails, and where it is superior.

Knowing the Competition

Gathering intelligence about the competition is almost as important as gathering intelligence about your own product. You can do it much the same way you study your own product and estimate its advantages and benefits.

Even though you do not generally invade the competition's camp to study the product from the standpoint of the engineers who made it, you can inundate yourself with the printed sales literature and advertising your competitor puts out.

If possible, you should try out the competition and see how it works. Be as objective about this as you would be in examining and testing your own product. There is usually a great deal to be learned by trying out the competition. You may find hidden advantages that sometimes can be answered only by your own product.

A Little Private Investigation

You should be looking for hidden flaws as well as good points in the competition's product. I use the word "hidden" because most of the literature used to promote a product obviously does not mention any of its weak features.

Having studied your own product fully at first, you can appreciate its own good points in relation to the less good—or *poor*—points of the competition. Once you have uncovered any such details, incorporate comparisons between your product and the competition in your sales pitch.

Another source of information about the competition is your own prospects, or people of your acquaintance who have tried out the product. This is a fount of important data. People who like the competition will be challenging you to come up with answers to questions that put your own product in a bad light in comparison to the competition.

One word of advice: If you do find what you think is a flaw in the competition, find out if this flaw has been corrected or not before you mention it. All you have to do is determine whether or not a new model is in the works or has been produced yet. Even after you have used this information, continue to check the opposition's product to make sure it has not been corrected. (If it has been, simply drop the point from your own discussion.)

Profile of the Competition

You should make a miniature profile of the competition's product—not quite so detailed as the profile of your own, but with the salient facts listed.

Put the competitive product's name at the top of the sheet, and divide the page into three columns. Label the first column "Competition's Features," the second column "Competition's Disadvantages," and the third column "(Your Own) Product's Offsetting Benefits."

By the time you have prepared this profile of the competition, you should be in the process of trying to neutralize the competition's advantages that outshine your own product's advantages. This is perhaps one of the most difficult areas in which you have to work. It is obvious that the competition is going to be as good as your product and, in some aspects, maybe even better.

Challenge the competition's claims as specifically as possible and as honestly as possible. It never pays to make unfounded statements that detract from the competition's product. Facts and figures—and a bit of creative thinking—can usually neutralize or equal any advantages the competition has over your product.

For example, if you are going up against a stiff competitor with a product that in some ways is superior to the one you are selling, the best way to proceed is, first of all, to make a list of the advantages and disadvantages of both competing products.

Be fair about these pluses and minuses. Admit that several elements of your competitor's product *are* better than yours. Remember that there will certainly be good points to brag about in yours.

> *Note:* Never allow yourself to get into a defensive position about the superiority of the competition.

With the two lists in front of you, compare the better features of your product to the less effective features of the other. Then show the obvious advantages of your own product and discuss them in detail against the competition's disadvantages.

If the competitor's product is definitely better and is better known in the field, you may have to fall back on the time-honored ploy invented by Avis when it went up against Hertz, a midget against a giant in the field. Avis invented a slogan to get at Hertz, and made it stick: "We try harder." Make the same claim for your product.

The main point I am trying to make is this: in order to neutralize a competitor's superiority, you must know the product of the competition almost as well as you know your own, in case push comes to shove in the final stages of your sales interview. It is an absolute "no-no" to go into such an interview without the complete and honest facts about all your competitors' products.

SUPPORTIVE PRODUCT INFORMATION

Your knowledge of your product and its competition is essential to any kind of sales pitch you are planning to use. You should have at least a general impression of a number of other details you can use to help sell your product.

These include two important elements:

1. The history of the product
2. Its competitive position in the industry

The Product Backgrounder

Most public relations firms hired to promote any product prepare almost immediately what is called a "backgrounder" on each product that is manufactured. In this backgrounder, the important advantages of the product are enumerated, along with possible benefits to the consumer. However, before these points are reached, the typical backgrounder usually elaborates on a history and development of the product.

Such material is usually dramatically interesting, insomuch as it might detail the problems the product manufacturer solved in trying to develop the product into a marketable item. For salespersons trying to sell the product, this material is invaluable as a kind of supportive story to back up the product and to make it more dramatically exciting as an engrossing success story.

History humanizes the product. The story of its development makes the product seem almost like the hero in a fairy tale. Not only does history humanize the product, it makes it more meaningful and thus more desirable to the consumer.

THE WOODSMAN WHO GOT COLD FEET

He was a Down Easter, born in Maine in 1872, one of the last of the small-time New England tinkerers and outdoorsmen. He grew up to run a dry-goods store; "dry goods" was supposed to refer to those articles for sale that were not "wet goods," that is, vegetables, fruits, meats, etc. In other words, he had himself a small convenience store.

Mostly, he loved to hunt. As much as he loved to hunt and slog through woods and marshes, fields and bogs, he *hated* to get his feet cold and wet. Given the out-of-doors game he was playing, it was impossible for him *not* to get his feet soaked and frozen every time he ventured outside.

One day as he sat trying to dry out his socks over a fire so he could get his boots back on again, one of the socks caught fire and burned up. He made a vow that he would never go out into the wet again without boots that would keep his feet dry and warm at the same time.

Tinkering in his shop, he came up with a pair of odd-looking galoshes made of rubber and leather—rubber to keep the water out and leather to keep the warmth in.

These Boots Are Made for Hunting

It was a terrific breakthrough. He now hunted with dry and warm feet. And he put his boots on sale at his dry-goods store. They went like hot cakes. Everybody wanted to hunt dry and warm. He was a hero in his own hometown.

Until . . .

Right. Pretty soon the leather parted company with the rest of the boots. When his customers found this out, they turned on him. Nobody would buy boots in his shop anymore. In fact, they boycotted it.

He hired a cobbler to correct the faults in his dry boots, and finally got a model that worked. They were good. But now too many people were suspicious of the product and wouldn't buy anything at all from him.

Then he got another idea. He had a good product. Why not sell it somewhere else? Siberia? Alaska? Or, maybe, someplace in Maine where nobody had ever heard his name before.

For Sale to Strangers Only

He made up a mailing list of people who might be interested and began advertising his boots by mail. Direct mail solicitation soon paid off. He began getting orders to supply a number of big stores in Massachusetts, New Hampshire, Vermont, Rhode Island, and Connecticut, as well as the more remote regions of Maine.

His store became a great success. By the time he died in 1967, his store—it was called "L. L. Bean's" after his name—truly was one of the biggest in the Maine area.

Today the store sells not by direct mail but by catalog, and it sells almost all articles of clothing in addition to the waterproof boots that almost buried L. L. Bean in a mountain of resentment and hate mail.

MAKING HISTORY AN EXCITING ADVENTURE

Your product may not have a built-in dramatic appeal like L. L. Bean's did, but I'd advise you to do the best you can to research the background of the company you represent in order to come up with an interesting story of the product and the people who make it. There are all kinds of human interest details you can weave into any factual history. It always helps to humanize a company and/or the product in order to make either desirable—and sought after—by your prospective buyer.

You may also find some colorful or inventive use of the product in your researches. If you are lucky, and the product was used in some important event in history, make a point of that fact!

> EXAMPLE: You are selling carbonated beverages, among which is the product called root beer. It was deliberately developed as a new drink to refresh the palates of visitors to the 1872 Philadelphia Exposition by Charles Elmer Hires. And, did you know that it was originally called "root tea," until Hires was enjoined to change "tea" to "beer" so as not to offend the masculine prerogatives of the attending American males?

COMPETITIVE POSITION IN THE INDUSTRY

You must always keep in mind the exact position of your product in relation to all its competitors. It is always necessary to keep in mind the feeling of confidence—or the lack of confidence—your product's position engenders in the customer. A product that is number ninety-nine in a field of ninety-nine has two and a half strikes against it to begin with.

The best way to play such a position is to point out that you are selling a superior but little-known product dominated by a number of well-established names in the field. However, don't fall into the trap of overplaying the superiority of your product. Be modest but firm.

The way to point up an unknown product is to select its main feature and exploit that to the hilt. You'll have to use your imagination and invent plausible reasons for the product's use. The more inventive you become, the more likely you are to arouse people's interest.

If you are lucky and are selling a product that is Number One, you simply roll with the wave of strength you come into the field with. That does not mean that you can afford to get careless. You must know your product well; you must know all your competition well. If yours is Number One, your customer will know that. But your prospect may not know *why* your product is Number One. That is up to you to demonstrate. Make sure to capitalize on your Number One position quietly but positively during every minute of your sales conversation.

The famous Avis and Hertz battle played an interesting ploy when Avis came out to counteract Hertz's obvious Number One position: "We're Number Two, but we try harder."

I had a good friend in the advertising business when that catchy line became popular and made Avis a real contender. My friend was appalled at the reverse audacity of the statement; it went completely against the grain of his advertising instincts. And yet it did put Avis on the map. Where it remains to this day.

KNOW YOUR SUPPORT STAFF

You must also be knowledgeable about a number of sales support services your product may have at its disposal. I refer to services the company supplies or makes available to its customers in conjunction with the product it sells.

For example:

1. Advertising programs
2. Consultation and evaluation
3. Credit provisions
4. Design services
5. Employee training
6. Financial services
7. Installation
8. Instructions for use
9. Maintenance and repair
10. Merchandising support
11. Resale assistance
12. Sales literature and catalogs
13. Sales promotion programs
14. Shipping and delivery
15. Studies and recommendations
16. Technical and inspection

Although this list is long, you will probably be able to find a certain number of these functions that your own company provides for its customers. Remember that service of any kind is a major marketing tool to help you sell products, ensure their proper use, and create maximum customer satisfaction.

You may quite properly use one of these support services in order to land an order in a critical selling situation. Service is so common that most people may not think about it as an advantage for the buyer of a product. It is a good idea to remind your prospect that the service is there for his or her use.

The service ploy is particularly valuable when your product is almost equal to your main competitor's. By adding a service that is valuable to a customer, you can sometimes overcome the prospect's hesitation, and sell the product because of the advantage supplied by the service.

Three Steps to Service Advantage

There are three steps you should take in utilizing this service feature in your sales interviews:

1. You must become thoroughly familiar with the sales support services provided by your company or available through your company.
2. You must learn how to utilize these services as effective tools for sales, employing this support service to make the sale in competitive situation.
3. You must remember to keep your prospects informed about these services because they are part of your own grab bag of tricks to help make sales.

PHYSICAL CHARACTERISTICS

Although a knowledge of the physical measurements and performance details of a product are an elementary requirement for anyone trying to sell it, you must continually refresh your memory on these most important details. Not knowing them at some crucial stage of a sales interview can prove not only to be highly embarrassing, but disastrous as well.

Here is a list of details with which you should be completely familiar:

Clauses and provisions
Colors, textures, and finishes
Composition
Guarantees
Limits of utility
Packaging
Payment details

Performance variations
Prices and discounts
Quality variations
Sizes and weights
Specification details
Terms of sale
Types, models, and designs

You should have all this information well memorized and stashed in your head so that you can bring it up for instant recall. It never hurts to have the information written down for quick consultation, either. You can get these details in product description bulletins and manuals prepared by the manufacturer for the use of the sales staff.

HOW MUCH AND HOW QUICK?

The most sensitive of all types of information relating to any product or service is the price and the payment policy. First of all, it is, obviously, the main purpose of the entire sales performance. At the same time, its revelation is the most serious and unnerving of the entire presentation.

In the final analysis, it is the price related to the product's quality, the competition, the product's performance, its availability, delivery, and a lot of other details that will help you achieve a sale or cause you to lose a sale.

Consider the matter from the point of view of the company that manufactures the product. The price must be right. If it's too high, the company loses. If it's too low, there's no profit. Thus there are stringent limitations imposed on product pricing and sales policies. While it is impractical to go into detail about the many different kinds of pricing that are used in selling these days, there are a few points that can be defined and explained.

CASH DISCOUNTS. These are relatively simple, but must be stated at the outset of a sales discussion so that there is no confusion between the seller and buyer.

F.O.B. PRICES. F.O.B. means "free on board." These prices have to do with shipping costs.

✓ F.O.B. TRUCK—SHIPPING POINT means that the cost of loading the goods on the truck at the seller's shipping point is to be paid by the buyer.

✓ F.O.B. CAR—DESTINATION means that the price includes loading into a railroad car at the seller's plant and the transportation charges to the ultimate destination. The seller is responsible for any loss or damage to the goods during transit.

✓ F.O.B. CAR—SHIPPING POINT, FREIGHT ALLOWED means that the price includes payment of transportation by the seller, but damage to the goods is the responsibility of the buyer.

GUARANTEED PRICE. This is an expression used when a buyer is given a set price for a limited time when market prices are fluctuating. It protects the buyer from loss due to such shifts.

LIST PRICE. This is a published price of a product subject to various discounts used when computing a buyer's actual cost. Price modifications are effected through changes in discounts from the list price. Discount levels are adjusted to answer changes in market conditions. Printed discount sheets are provided for confidential use. List prices seldom include shipping costs.

NET PRICE. This represents the customer's price after any allowable discounts or other deductions have been subtracted from the list price, but before addition of transportation costs, taxes, and so on.

ZONE PRICE. This is a price that applies for all sales within a specific geographic area. A major market may be divided into a number of zones. This method is used when the transportation charge is not a dominant factor and the sales volume is substantial.

3

Preparation for the Successful Closing: II. Know Your Prospect

Next in importance to a total knowledge of the product you're selling is a reasonable indication that the prospect you are planning to sell has a specific or general use for the product. The age-old wheeze about the "super" salesperson puts a neat reverse English on the principle of "qualifying the prospect": "He's such a good salesman he could sell refrigerators to the Eskimos," or, "He's such a good salesman he could sell fur coats to the Bedouins." And so forth and so on.

The reverse English makes for a good joke or simply acts to focus attention on a salesperson's ability to stimulate a buyer into wanting a product even if he or she may not want or need it. The straight shot of "qualifying a prospect" is the determination by the salesperson that the buyer is indeed in need of a particular product and whether or not he or she can afford it.

Qualification in this sense simply means that the seller must determine a careful and accurate profile of the prospective buyer along several specific lines:

- Does he/she own the product already?
- Does he/she need the product?
- Can he/she afford the product?

THE STORY OF JASON DEANE

Jason Deane sold boats. He sold powerboats, he sold inboards, he sold windsurfers, he sold yachts, and he sold superyachts. He sold many more small boats than large ones, but he knew the differences in price, the differences in performance, the differences in the aura created by a superyacht and a sleek little powerboat.

In his office overlooking the yacht harbor, Jason kept a large file of his clients. Whenever he heard something about one of his boat owners, he wrote it down and filed it in his master file. Whenever he read something about one of his clients, he clipped it and put it carefully away.

In addition to his filing system, Jason kept a line of communication open between himself and his clients by an occasional telephone call, even after he had sold them a product. "Just called to see how everything was going, Mr. Thompson." And so on and so forth.

One of his clients was named Barron. Tim Barron had purchased a very small seagoing yacht from Jason three years ago. Barron was working his way up the corporate ladder at a large manufacturing plant in Connecticut. His career unfortunately had been on hold for some years now, and Jason knew that Barron was getting fidgety in his job, hoping for some kind of advance. But with the stock market plunge and the junk bond fiasco, his corporation was keeping things on a tight rein.

Data for the File Cabinet

One morning Jason saw a notice in the paper to the effect that Tim Barron had been promoted to advertising manager of the corporation where he worked. He filed it immediately in the Barron package. Not a week later he was reading a newsletter from a real-estate firm and again spotted Barron's name; he had just purchased a large estate house in the posh section of Greenwich, Connecticut.

It was a bright Saturday morning and the sun glistened on the water outside Jason's window. He dialed Tim Barron and was soon chatting with him.

"Haven't heard from you, Tim, and wondered how your yacht was making out."

"Fine, Jason, fine. We love it. No complaints, you know."

"Reason I asked, I just happened to acquire a beautiful, well-kept 80-footer, and wondered if you'd like to take a look at it."

Forgive Jason for that slight fib. He had been keeping the 80-footer for some time now, unable to move it. But now. . . .

"I don't think so, Jason," Tim Barron responded. "Nothing wrong with the one I've got, is there?"

"Not at all, Tim. But I did want you to look this one over. It's got a kind of elegance you don't often see."

Tim chuckled. "Tell you what. I'm going down to the marina to putter around mine this afternoon. If you drop by, maybe I could see my way free to take a look."

Jason hung up, smiling faintly.

A Diamond In a Bright Blue Setting

Immediately he checked over the 80-footer, ordered one of his assistants to make sure it was spic and span, and then had it moved from the spot it occupied to the jutting point of the marina where it seemed to stand alone in all its splendor. By midafternoon, the sun would begin sinking, and it would be almost like a diamond glistening in the setting of the blue water and the yacht basin behind it.

Tim was scraping paint when Jason climbed aboard his little 40-footer. After the usual exchange of amenities, Tim brought out beers from a cooler and opened two. "Now where's this big new thing you're so proud of?" he asked.

Jason turned and waved the beer can in the direction of the sparkling sea. "She's right over there, Tim."

Tim glanced across the water. "Which one is it? I mean, counting left or right from that beauty that's riding the water out there?"

"Tim," Jason said softly. "That's it."

Tim's eyes widened. "Wow."

In seconds they were walking to the dock where Jason had his powerboat. And in minutes they were aboard the 80-footer, wandering around the superbly furnished interior.

Jason said not much of anything. But what he did say made a great deal of sense to Tim Barron.

"It's nowhere near as big as Donald Trump's *Trump Princess*," he said with a smile.

Tim shrugged. "I heard Donald outgrew her anyway."

"People do outgrow the things they own," Jason murmured.

Tim looked at him.

A Little Competition

They strolled along the deck. Tim's face as animated. His eyes sparkled. He took a deep breath and drew in the sea air.

"I've got a man coming over to see her tomorrow," Jason said in an offhand fashion.

"You do?" Tim's face stiffened.

"Not hard to sell a beauty like this one."

Tim moved around the deck like a man composing a difficult sonnet in his head. He came back to stand by Jason. "How much?"

Jason smiled. "Maybe you don't want to know, Tim."

"Maybe I do!" snapped Tim, suddenly serious.

Jason told him.

Tim blinked, but then straightened, like a boxer recovering after a hard blow to the solar plexis. "Listen. Don't sell this baby until I get back to you."

Jason took a deep breath. "But, Tim. Are you serious? I don't want to hold up on a practically firm deal."

Tim pointed his forefinger at Jason's chest and stabbed it three times. "I'll be back to you tomorrow!"

Jason nodded. "I promise."

Closing Time

The next day Tim Barron and his wife and three teenage children boarded the 80-footer and made the usual conversation with Jason Deane. By the end of the afternoon Tim Barron had signed a binder and paid it by check.

Jason deposited the check to his account on Monday with a smile. He had certainly done his homework on that deal. The 80-footer had been at anchor for a long time. Just waiting for a prospect. And the prospect had appeared suddenly in Jason's filing system.

Once Jason had put the prospect together with the product, the product had practically *sold itself*—although there is no such thing as a product that sells itself. No. Jason had sold the prospect because he *knew his prospect inside out*. In effect, he had thoroughly qualified the prospect before he had decided on a product to sell him.

The truth of the matter is that at least one half of closing depends not on the actual closing itself, but on the *preliminary qualification* of the prospect. Qualification is not in any way an exploration of your chances to land a client; *chance* has nothing to do with it. Qualification is the process of finding out what the prospect already has in his possession, what his or her future plans may be, what the prospect may need to fulfill those plans, and in what manner your product will suit and benefit him or her.

HOW TO QUALIFY A PROSPECT

The question immediately arises: "What is the best way to qualify a prospect?"

The answer is not a simple one. It is complex, but essential to a successful closing, or, better yet, to all successful closings.

Qualification of a prospect breaks down into six different parts:

1. Determine what your prospect owns now.
2. Determine the price range your prospect can handle.
3. Determine what feature he or she *likes* about the product or service.
4. Determine what *improvement* over his or her current product is desired.
5. Determine if there are hidden obstacles in the way of a sale.
6. Determine at least two or three choices to present.

And then get to work and find out the facts about your prospect. How? By asking questions of people—that's how.

Gathering Intelligence

Everybody has an itch to know what the other person *has*, how much he or she is worth, what their living rooms look like, whether they spend their spare time in the summer on their boat or at their lake. You can find out a great deal about other people by the simple expedient of casual conversation.

A good general rule for the gathering of intelligence is to accomplish it without making too many waves. That is, a prospect who becomes aware that someone is trying to find out details about his or her life can become unnerved and simply run away, or, worse yet, close the door on you.

The people close to your prospect are the people who know him or her best. They act as a buffer to protect him or her from nosiness. However, if you are a good intelligence gatherer you can turn this protectionism to your own profit by the judicious use of casual curiosity and perhaps your indulgence in just a bit of gossip.

When you visit a prospect, the first person you see is usually the receptionist. Don't sit around flipping through magazines while the receptionist phones your prospect to say that you are waiting. Talk to her or him. The receptionist is usually a fount of information about the division of the company in which she or he serves, and about the people in it.

After the receptionist, there is the personal secretary of your prospect. She, or he, can also become a conduit of information about your prospect. Be friendly to these people. By letting out a little about yourself, you can get them to open up to you a little about themselves, and then, when you are on a friendlier basis, you can move to your objective—which is to find out all you can about your prospect.

A Little Detective Work

Detectives in fiction are usually seen as snoops. But you are not really a snoop. You are gathering valuable information about a prospect who may someday become your client. Do not be afraid to find out things about other people. Even if you are caught or brought up short for your snooping, you may find out that your prospect is more flattered about your interest than alarmed by your persistence.

There are also sources of information you can develop. Businesspersons who deal with your prospect generally know quite a lot about his or her life and personal affairs. You should handle these sources of information in a subtle way, of course—not making it obvious that you are on an investigative hunt for "all the facts."

Remember: An ounce of discretion is worth a pound of crudity.

The following major headings indicate the six steps to qualifying a prospect. Know them by heart before you begin.

DETERMINE WHAT YOUR PROSPECT OWNS NOW

A good field general depends on intelligence reports in order to estimate the strength of his opponent. A good salesperson likewise must know exactly what his prospect already has in order not to try to sell something already owned. By knowing what your prospect already has, you can determine several other important points about him: the kind of person he or she is; how the prospect feels about the product; what the prospect lacks and needs.

The Kind of Person He or She Is

If your prospect keeps an office or department that is run haphazardly and inefficiently on cheap and inferior equipment, you know that basically that person tends to buy cheap rather than expensive.

However, this does not mean that you should not try to persuade him or her to buy a more expensive and more efficient product or service. After all, the prospect may have inherited a rundown department. Or, business may have just picked up and the prospect is hoping to expend money to bring his department up to scratch.

How the Prospect Feels About the Product

What the prospect already has in use in his office or department can tell you a great deal. It is a definite tip-off to the character and attitude of the prospect.

I am reminded of that saying in the diet ads: "You are what you eat."

A prospective buyer can be identified and characterized very accurately by what he owns, by the products he has, by the way he uses them.

In order words, to paraphrase the diet statement for our purposes here in this book: "You are what you *own*."

What the Prospect Lacks and Needs

Your prospect may not even know that he or she lacks a product or service that will help. You can see the deficit immediately when you view the prospect's environment.

You should pounce on such a gap and mention it. Then you should push your product and explain how it would take care of the prospect's needs.

On the other hand, your prospect may know exactly what he or she lacks, having learned that such a vacuum does exist in equipment or service.

Treat your discovery not as an aloof put-down, but as a tip to a friend.

How to Find Out What a Prospect Owns

There are a number of different ways in which to determine the products and services in an office or department. The traditional method involves a visit to the prospect with a chance to look around. You can always ask questions about how this works, or how that works. Most businesspersons are happy to explain things to people who don't understand exactly how things work.

If you find a reticent prospect—they *do* exist—simply keep asking questions without being pushy. You may be able to soften him or her up enough to get some response. Meanwhile, while you are talking, continue to look around in a casual way to determine some of the answers yourself.

You can also make use of secondary sources of information, as has already been discussed: receptionists, secretaries, coworkers, delivery personnel, members of the family. And so on.

Fast Food—Fast Sale

It was one of those hot August days, and the atmosphere had turned into a pressure cooker. I was wilted and stumbled into a cheap eatery, one of those brightly illuminated, formica-gleaming, chrome-shining emporiums dedicated to instant gluttony.

I was trying to cool off with a glass of iced tea before the ice all vanished into the air, and I noticed an attractive woman at the next table deep in conversation with her companion, an older woman who kept dabbing at her forehead with a napkin to sop up the perspiration.

". . . won't do a thing," the young woman was saying, shaking her head. "This heat just seemed to blow it out. It won't work. I have to take four reams of paper to that place across the street."

"But that's expensive!" said the older woman.

"I know," wailed the woman. "But we've got to get the mailing out."

"Can't you get a replacement?"

"We don't want *that machine* again!" snapped the woman. She named the product, pointing out that it was always going on the fritz.

I knew the product: a good copier, but obviously not able to take care of the heavy schedule the woman expected it to handle. Now *I* was representing a product. . . .

Going on Surveillance

I followed her out of the fast-food joint and once in her building pretended to be looking for an office down the hall from hers. A moment after she had gone in her place, I was in there, giving her my name and product.

"Isn't that a coincidence!" she cried.

I agreed.

One of my lucky closings. I had qualified a client before I had even imagined the prospect lived.

There's a moral here somewhere.

DETERMINE THE PRICE RANGE YOUR PROSPECT CAN HANDLE

The amount of money the prospect is able to come up with for your product or service is one of the trickiest considerations you will have to deal with. It is never wise to underestimate the amount of money any client is willing to come up with—especially for a product he or she may *really* want. Nor is it wise to overestimate the amount.

Determining the price range takes a bit of detective work. You can generally determine the solvency of a company by looking it up in Dun and Bradstreet, or by checking it out with someone who works there or knows someone who works in the company.

There is no surefire way to determine the viable figure you can set for a product, but you must make some kind of stab at it. If it's guesswork, you will always be aware of that when you come to your interview and its closing. Then you can generally put forward your ball-park figure—this one strictly off the top of the head, as I have said—and move up from that or down from that until you hit a happy medium.

How to Bracket the Proper Figure

Here's the general idea in coming up with the correct figure for a closing. I go into the interview with a guesswork figure in mind. The big question finally comes up: "How much?"

In answer to that, you *never* say: "Well, it actually costs $1,500, but don't forget, that's with this and that and so on. . . ."

Ahah! It's $1,500, and goodbye to you, Norman-baby!

SEARCH AND DESTROY: "Most any buyer of a machine with all the features I've mentioned and the benefits you are aware of would probably be prepared to spend at least $1,500 for it. Of course, those fortunate few who have plenty of money and don't have to worry about what they spend, would probably pay about $2,000 to $3,000. For those on a limited budget—and who isn't these days?—you would have to stay at about $1,250. Where do you fit in this range?"

"Well, about $1,500."

CLOSING ATTACK: "It's fantastic to think that this machine you're looking at has all the features you want, and that it only involves $1,250— really $250 under the amount you've been thinking of!"

Let's analyze this for a moment.

First of all, the numbers require a preliminary guess of what the prospect *might* be considering: in this case, $1,500. Second, the prospect really has no figure in mind at all. But when the prospect studies the brackets you've indicated, he wimps it out right in the middle. You've already raised the amount past the price of your product in figuring $1,500, so it is obvious that the prospect feels happy to have avoided all those high figures. The inflated figures of $2,000 and $3,000, are just there, of course, for window dressing. They make the prospect feel good by being able to avoid them.

Should the prospect select the bottom figure, you simply alter your "closing attack" statement to: "Which is exactly what you planned to spend."

The Triple-Threat Gambit

The triple-threat gambit is particularly useful when you sense that your prospect is hedging on paying the high price he or she thinks the product is going to cost. Determining whether or not a prospect is skittish pricewise is difficult at best.

Some salespersons can instinctively tell when a prospect is panicking over the number of dollars he or she must spend. Those not endowed with that kind of instinct have to work harder at it.

A close study of the prospect is usually enough. There may be signs of nervousness, an inability to maintain eye contact with you, evasive shiftings of the body, much clearing of the throat, and staring at the ceiling.

The prospect who shows this kind of nervousness is someone you will have to handle carefully. When you feel that the prospect is hauling in the reins on the deal because of the money involved, proceed with the following five steps of the triple-threat gambit:

1. Start out by stating a number that is about one fifth again above your target price. (Multiply by 120 percent, if you think that's easier.) Once you have selected and stated that figure, elaborate on the idea to your prospect by pointing out that most people—"everybody else, why not you?"—will probably be *ready* to pay at least the number that is your target price.

2. Double your target price itself, adding in a figure between the target price and its double to help the figures along. And elaborate: "A fortunate few can pay this figure," and name twice your target figure. This will blow the mind of the prospect; it's way too high, and he or she is beginning to perspire already.

3. Wind up the triple-threat spiel with your target figure. "And there are those on a limited or fixed budget who can't go over this figure," and that's your target figure. Now the prospect begins to relax. In fact, relief is evident. The face lights up. The eyes brighten. You can see the positive signs.

4. The triple-bracket gambit has been played, and it's simply a matter now of letting it spin its way out. No more figures. You let the imprint of the figures sink in, saying absolutely nothing for a while, and then you smile and you come out with the big question: "Which suits you?"

5. When the prospect comes out either with the target figure or the low figure, you reply in the proper fashion, and then smile once again. You and the prospect are on the same wavelength. All's right with the world. And you say, "Isn't it *fantastic* to think that the machine you're looking at is the one. . . ."

DETERMINE WHAT FEATURE HE OR SHE *LIKES*

The third phase in qualifying the prospect involves one of the most important considerations in the process: determining what the prospect *likes* about the product or service you are selling. If the product does not have what the buyer *likes*, it's pointless to try to sell it.

DETERMINE WHAT *IMPROVEMENT* THE PROSPECT WANTS

No product is ever completely perfect for any prospect. There is always something missing, or something that the product does not quite do to perfection. Perhaps there are two or three features lacking. By the time the product has been in use for several years, the prospect may be looking around for a new model to exchange it for.

You find out about these needs by discussing business with your prospects, even after you have closed with them. You can do this either by making one-on-one visits, or by discussing business on the telephone.

Sometimes you can get leads on prospects from satisfied buyers. It is always a good practice to revisit your satisified customers once in a while. During give-and-take about conditions and the way things are, you frequently are able to pick up important details about other people—friends of your customer.

> "Bill Humphreys needs a lot more speed in that copier he has. He's got a five-hundred-page manuscript he needs copied—and his secretary is spending hours there feeding in pages by hand. *He* could use a bigger machine. Isn't there one that grips each page and feeds it in automatically?"

Of course there is! And you call up Bill Humphreys and tell him about it and you've got a sale.

DETERMINE IF THERE ARE HIDDEN OBSTACLES

Your prospect may be the head of his or her department, and yet perhaps the prospect must get approval from the board of directors, or someone equally off to the side but important in the structure of the company.

I've learned to proceed with caution, especially if I am putting on a dog and pony show that is a big and exhaustive demonstration.

You feel like saying: "This is complicated and I'm not about to pull it off just so you can say it's got to go to the board for approval!"

What you *do* say is something along these lines:

> "If we're fortunate enough today to find the proper model of the product, are you in a position to proceed with a closing?"

Psychologically, you have taken the monkey off the back of the prospect so that he can admit:

> "Before we go any further, our board of directors does have to meet and approve it."

On the other hand, the answer may be, "I'm in a position to close with you."

Three cheers!

DETERMINE TWO OR THREE CHOICES TO PRESENT

Supersalesperson Ed McMahon, Johnny Carson's sidekick for years and years, started out as a pitchman on a boardwalk. That is, he began his career selling things of all kinds.

He loved working one-on-one with people, and he could sell anything he wanted to.

One of his rules of the game always interested me a great deal. Here are his very words, from his autobiography:

> One time I set up a counter for a dealer who offered many different colored fountain pens. I told him, "I want red and green. Don't give me any other colors." He couldn't understand that, but I wanted to limit the choices. In my pitch, there was a point where I asked the customer, "If you were to buy this pen, would you prefer the red one or the green one?" So they've got to make a choice. Let's say the customer answered, "Red is my favorite color." I'd say, "I am awfully fond of red myself. Let me just put this red pen in your hand. Would you write with it and see how it feels?" Eliminating choices is very important. You don't offer [a lot of] things to sell, just a couple.

The supersalesperson is right. Eliminating choices is mandatory. That's why all manufacturers fight for choice spots in supermarkets. The consumer is inundated with products to the left and right. There are too many choices to make. However, given only Number One and Number Two, it's a lot simpler to decide: I'll take corn flakes instead of Rice Krispies.

The Psychological Imperative

Charles Dickens, the great British novelist, died in 1870, just after he had begun a novel titled *The Mystery of Edwin Drood*. When his publisher located the unfinished manuscript, he wanted another writer to complete the work, but Dickens had not written down an outline of what he intended the end to be.

The actual murderer—for the novel was to be a murder mystery within the crime genre—was not named at all. It was a matter of guesswork as to whodunit, to use the argot of the mystery lover.

Through the years a number of ambitious novelists did

indeed *finish* Dickens's novel, using different solutions to the mystery, each with logical murder outlines.

Drood as a Musical Comedy

When Rupert Holmes decided to produce the play on Broadway, he made it into a musical comedy, with the following interesting wrinkle:

There was no ending, with a solution worked out and explained onstage. Instead, all the actors who could have been the murderer lined up across the stage at the end of the play, with the stage manager (a character in the stage version) passing along in back of them and holding his hand over each prospective murderer. The audience, by its applause, indicated which one it thought was the killer.

In a discussion with Holmes one night, he told me that the identity of the murderer varied from performance to performance. They would make it a habit of changing the lineup, because it soon became obvious that none of the characters *on the extreme ends* would ever be selected. It would always be someone on the *inside*, usually toward the end of the group. Never Number One or Number Seven!

Psychologically Speaking

For some reason, the human psyche *wants* to choose the medium state, the less spectacular, the more moderate.

It is up to you to give the prospective consumer perhaps three models to choose from—with the fact firmly in mind that the middle one will prevail!

4

The Art of Conversation Control

THINGS, ACTIONS—THEN REFINEMENTS

Speech began historically with grunts and groans and hisses, with each grouping of such sounds, called phonemes, signifying an *object* of some kind. Later, this progressed to groups of phonemes signifying an *action*. Then, the combination of things and acts became a larger umbrella of communication. Soon these two main elements were further fragmented and refined into more complex grammatical arrangements, with word groupings indicating various *kinds* of objects, and various *subtypes* of actions.

But always, in the background, there was that subliminal purpose for speech: the attempt to *control*.

52

"Come here, Johnny!"
"Eat your vegetables!"
"Put on your rubbers!"

THE SUBLIMINAL IMPERATIVE

So far I have dealt strictly with affirmative comments in the indicative mood with instructions and orders in the imperative. Here the attempt at control is overt and unconcealed. But in other forms, the attempt to control can be implicit rather than explicit:

"You'll burn yourself in that sun without lotion."
"They've sighted sharks beyond the pier."
"Deadline for term papers is Friday."

Note that in each of these bland statements of fact there is a hidden persuader.

"You'll burn yourself in that sun without lotion. *(Don't go outdoors unless you put on a sun screen.)*"
"They've sighted sharks beyond the pier. *(Stay out of the water today.)*"
"Deadline for term papers is Friday. *(If you miss the deadline, you'll flunk the course.)*"

Nevertheless, each of these statements stands on its own, even with the subliminal instruction or warning unstated. That is, there is no need for you to respond to any of those three statements, any more than there was a need to respond to the three in the preceding section.

COMMUNICATION IS A TWO-WAY STREET

Humankind soon enough realized that communication was a two-way street, and had to be so to be effective. One man standing in a group of a dozen might talk to great length, but if no one took up the conversation and responded to him, there was only a kind of lecture-like stasis achieved.

In fact, one of the very first refinements on speech, certainly evolved at its beginnings, was the interrogative mood. Thus the conventional greeting of one human being to another was couched originally, and remains to this day, in the form of a question.

"Hello. *How are you?*"
"*What's new?*"
"*How goes it?*"

Even in foreign languages, the same format holds true:

"*Comment allez-vous?*"
"*¿Cómo está usted?*"
"*Wie geht es Ihnen?*"

So important is the interrogative mood in Spanish that any question in a Spanish text begins with an inverted question mark to establish the fact that an interrogation is coming and ends with a question mark right-side-up to indicate that the question has been asked.

In effect, the user of the interrogative mood actually exerts immediate control of the communication by hanging a question in the air that must be answered. A question tends to upset the status quo of the conversational dynamic enough to *demand* some kind of response.

HOW TO CONTROL COMMUNICATION

There are three ways to control a verbal exchange in either a conversation or an interview:

1. By a direct order (imperative mood)
2. By an order understood by the stated facts (indicative mood)
3. By a question (interrogative mood)

In the case of a conversation with someone on your own level of sophistication and intelligence, the "direct order" in the imperative is almost totally eschewed. It still smacks of the kindergarten, the nursery room, or of the kitchen table:

"Sit up straight."
"Wash your hands."
"Eat your broccoli."

In the case of the "understood" order in the indicative, it is quite possible that in a spirited or heated conversation, such an implication that is not stated outright can be ignored, misunderstood, or simply assumed not to exist.

The word "understood" itself is, thus, an anomaly. Watch out for this type of construction. A wily conversationist can use it to deflect the line of discussion and sabotage any value you might have wanted to call attention to.

It is the direct question in the interrogative that has become the handiest tool for anyone interested in the art of persuasion. Essentially a question almost of necessity *forces* an answer in the direct flow of the conversation.

ANALYZING AN EARLIER EXCHANGE

For the moment let's back up to what I was talking about in Chapter 1—the closing that I had inadvertently blown. Here's the way the exchange went:

HIM: Can you deliver after ten days' notice?
ME: No problem.

As I have pointed out, my analysis of the gaffe showed that I should have come back at my prospect with a question in turn:

HIM: Can you deliver after ten days' notice?
ME: Shall I have it sent to the main office or to the branch we were talking about?

You can see the dynamics of the exchange. In the first, the dynamics of the conversation reaches a point of equilibrium. The question, "Can you deliver after ten days' notice?" leaves the conversation hanging in the air. After any question there is automatic suspense generated until the question is answered. When I thoughtlessly responded, "No problem," I inadvertently neutralized the suspense. There was no reason for the conversation to continue.

My prospect was quite right in saying what he did say: "Good. I'll be in touch." In other words, "So long."

Even an answer of "no" would have been better than what I said. With a "no" the dynamics of the exchange would have *suggested* further explanation. "No. But I can do it in eleven days"—or some such.

What we are dealing with here is an exercise in give-and-take, a process of strophe and antistrophe, a tennis lob and a return, a thrust and a counterthrust. Once the dynamics of any verbal exchange is neutralized or dies down, you have lost control of the interview—and the sale, of course.

A DIGRESSION INTO SEMANTICS

There is an ancient joke that was making the rounds during the Great Depression of the 1930s. I have to explain the circumstances, or the two-liner I am about to relate makes no sense. In fact, there is history in the simple use of the term "two-liner." Everyone today knows that a "one-liner" is a joke of one or two sentences uttered by a stand-up comic.

In those days, most jokes were told onstage, or on the radio, usually by two, rather than one, person. There was the comic and the stooge. The joke was the punchline of the series of exchanges between the two.

When the print media took up this form of jest, it usually involved two lines of printed give-and-take:

> STOOGE: Who was that lady I saw you walking down the street with last night?
> COMIC: That was no lady. That was my wife.

Or, a variation that fits the modern scene even better than the original:

STOOGE: Who was that lady I saw you walking down the street with last night?
COMIC: That was no lady. That was my brother George. He just walks that way.

During the Depression, as I was saying a few paragraphs back, there was a very popular two-liner that went:

STOOGE: How do you spell the word "embarrassed"?
COMIC: E-m-b-a-r-r-a-s-s-e-d. And you spell the other word f-i-n-a-n-c-i-a-l-l-y.

Financially embarrassed. Two words that went together like Scotch and soda. A modern pairing of words such as that might bring up a current two-liner:

STOOGE: How do you spell the word "intercourse"?
COMIC: I-n-t-e-r-c-o-u-r-s-e. And you spell the other word s-e-x-u-a-l.

Because of this close linkage between the word "intercourse" and "sexual" in the modern mind, it has almost completely put the damper on the use of the word "intercourse" in polite conversation. Unfortunately, intercourse is the word I feel most adequately conveys the feeling of give-and-take in a conversation between two people, particularly in an exchange between businesspersons and or salespersons and prospects.

Thus, while I did hesitate to use the word "intercourse" for the reason I have mentioned, I now use it. First of all, let's look at the meaning of "intercourse" in its more general sense. It comes from the Latin words "inter" (between) and "course" (flowing), that is, what flows between two people in an exchange or conversation.

THE DYNAMICS OF VERBAL INTERCOURSE

Now we are getting close to the real meaning of conversational dynamics. In verbal intercourse there is unceasing energy and movement; once either is lost, there is no conversation. In verbal intercourse there is also direction and indirection. It is up to the controller of the conversation to direct it—or misdirect it if need be.

Here is a diagram of a typical series of exchanges of dialogue in a sales interview:

SALESPERSON	PROSPECT
Greeting.	Greeting. Question 1.
Answer. Question 2.	Answer. Question 3.
Answer. Question 4.	Objection 1.
Answer. Question 5.	Objection 2.
Answer. Closing attempt 1.	Objection 3.
Answer. Question 6.	Answer. Question 7.
Answer. Closing attempt 2.	Objection 4.
Answer. Closing attempt 3.	Agreement.

We'll be looking at the technique of overcoming objections later on. A quick study of the diagram above shows you one thing very quickly and very clearly:

There are seven questions asked in a series of eight exchanges, in addition to the three closing attempts, which are usually couched in interrogative terms. The salesperson uses only interrogations throughout this exchange, for the greeting itself properly falls into that category—"How are you today?"—that waits for an answer.

Point: Questions are the cement that holds together the fabric of verbal intercourse.

Or how about this, as a golden rule for you to paste by your bathroom mirror:

> *Golden rule of business:* The question mark is the hook that catches the big fish in any business interview.

WHERE DO YOU FIND ENOUGH QUESTIONS TO ASK?

If you examine the use of language you can see that almost any statement made may be shifted into a question without too much difficulty. All it takes is a bit of ingenuity. Once you have gotten used to making the shift, it becomes second nature.

Let's take a classic case, probably the best-known sentence in the Western world:

In the beginning God created the heaven and the earth.

The atheist, or anti-Christian, might question that statement in this way:

Did God in the beginning create the heaven and the earth?

For the Christian, it's even easier:

In the beginning God created the heaven and the earth, didn't He?

Elementary, my dear Watson—isn't it?

Utilizing the "Confirmatory" Question

Technically, there is no conventional term to describe this add-on question; I have chosen to call it a "confirmatory" question, that is, the add-on question turns the statement into a "confirmatory" interrogation. The essential point is obvious: by couching a sentence now and then in this form, you are able to anticipate an answer of some kind from your respondent. Thus you can be assured at least that your prospect is still awake.

The confirmatory should not be overused. There's nothing worse than a series of statements winding up with that short pause and the inverted question hung onto the end. It becomes expected, and thus it becomes a joke. It's best to plot the confirmatory at the end of two or three sentences. This gives the prospect a chance to respond and you a chance to lead him on to your next point—provided there isn't a question of some kind from the prospect.

As Sherlock Holmes pointed out, this is all elementary stuff.

You can always place the confirmatory at the beginning of your statement, simply for variety and for effect. It's a lot clumsier, but it can sometimes prove effective.

Utilizing the "Reverse Confirmatory"

By a little judicious juggling, you can switch the confirmatory into a reverse position, that is, at the beginning of the statement rather than at the end:

Didn't God in the beginning create the heaven and the earth?

It's clumsier, but it can be effective.

Let's suppose you are selling fax machines. You could couch your confirmatory or your reverse confirmatory in the following manner:

CONFIRMATORY. "Most progressive companies today depend on a direct fax-machine line, wouldn't you say?"

REVERSE CONFIRMATORY. "Wouldn't you say that most progressive companies today depend on a direct fax-machine line hookup?"

Confirmatory III—The "Buried" Confirmatory

There's still another way to break up the monotony of the confirmatory. You can work it into the middle of the statement you want to get across. This is difficult when you work with our classic line, but you *could* do something like this:

> In the beginning—wouldn't you agree?—God created the heaven and the earth.

Not exactly a memorable line, but adequate. As for the fax sales pitch, how about this?:

> "Most progressive companies today, wouldn't you agree, depend on a direct fax-machine line."

HOW TO TURN STATEMENTS INTO QUESTIONS

The technique has been set up for you. It's up to you to get into the habit of breaking your sentences up into what may be a brand-new way for you. But it will help you to keep your prospect—your respondee—on the hook and not let him or her off until you *want* to ease the pressure.

How do you do it?

> SCENE: New York street.
> TOURIST: How do you get to Carnegie Hall?
> VIOLINIST: Practice. Practice. Practice.

And the violinist in that hoary old jape has just about summed it up. For working up your confirmatory questions you must drill yourself to think in the three ways I have mentioned. In some cases, you can use two of these techniques together to balance each other off. Do not allow monotony to creep into your speech patterns. There is nothing more noticeable than the use of one technique to exhaustion.

THE "RECONFIRMATORY" QUESTION

Although it is impossible to control what I call the reconfirmatory question, you should always be on the alert for it. The reason it is out of your control is that it must come from your respondee, from your prospect. It's simply a matter of luck.

In the fax situation, the prospect might have simply dropped a thought into the conversation in this manner:

"A progressive company today depends on a direct fax-machine line."

And of course this is the perfect point for a strong reconfirmatory. And you say:

"Doesn't it ever!"

This leaves you a perfect opening to say almost anything in your prepared presentation that you want to. Remember, even though you have couched the reconfirmatory in the form of a question, it's a rhetorical question at most. And it's a marvelous springboard for a good solid pitch to follow. The prospect has made the statement; when the prospect speaks, it *must* be true!; and what you are doing is confirming this feeling and slipping your own product spiel in under his nose so he cannot possibly miss it!

> *Note:* The confirmatory is a matter of simple luck. You cannot count on it. But you must be alert for it when it pops up. Then—make the most of it!

Making the Most of the Reconfirmatory

Let's suppose your prospect has inadvertently opened the floodgates wide to a reconfirmatory question and an affirmation plus.

PROSPECT: A progressive company today depends on a direct fax-machine line.

YOU: Doesn't it! When you speak to anyone about the fax phenomenon, you don't ask if he's got one, you ask him what kind he's got! And you want to tell him you've got the best, don't you?

PROSPECT: Well, yes.

YOU: The best *and* the most efficient. You can get all kinds, of course. But with ours, you'll be among the top customers of the new and necessary product. You don't depend on the mail service anymore, do you?

PROSPECT: Takes weeks to cross town.

YOU: And those messenger chaps—their charges are going through the roof—don't you think?

PROSPECT: Oh—yes.

YOU: You've simply got to have a fax to operate competitively, don't you?

PROSPECT: Uh—I suppose so.

YOU: Then aren't you glad we can look at exactly what you might need to keep your office expenses down and the speed of communication up?

And so on.

These are the four nuances of the confirmatory question, the most important tool in the repertoire of the interviewer. Practice them until they become second nature to you. You'll need a storehouse of them in your mind when you come to those most important last five minutes in any interview.

Remember the four "confirmatory" questions:

- The confirmatory question
- The reverse confirmatory question
- The hidden confirmatory question
- The reconfirmatory question

THE PING-PONG QUESTION

Have you ever found yourself in a conversation, as I have, with a person who sounds like an echo in the valley?

YOU: Are you making over thirty thousand a year?
OTHER: *Am* I making over thirty thousand a year?
YOU: That's what I asked. How much do you make?
OTHER: How much do I *make?*
YOU: Do you always repeat everything anyone asks you?
OTHER: Do I always *repeat* everything anyone asks me?
YOU: What kind of a conversation is this, anyway?
OTHER: A very informative one, I'm sure.

This kind of verbal intercourse is ridiculous, of course. But it leads to an interesting new type of question—a question that is similar in technique to the echo question above. For example:

PROSPECT: Is it possible to get the machine in beige?
YOU: Would getting the machine in beige satisfy your needs?

You can see that the technique is not definitely an echo. However, it *resembles* an echo in that the question originally asked is not really answered, but is lobbed back with another question welded onto it.

PROSPECT: Can I get delivery of the item in two weeks?
YOU: Does getting delivery of the item in two weeks suit your current needs?
PROSPECT: Yes, it does.
YOU: Then let's sign the papers now.

The advantage of the Ping-Pong question, which is what I call this double-edged technique, is that you don't actually cut yourself off from the sale if the answer happens to be no.

PROSPECT: Does this fax machine print in color?
YOU: Does its capacity to print in color meet your needs?
PROSPECT: No. I just wondered because I see no need to pay for some expensive feature I don't need.

You can figure out what would have happened if you had not used the Ping-Pong question here.

Warning: Do not overuse the Ping-Pong question. Never use it in a querulous or overbearing manner. Do not make it sound like the echo question discussed above. If you seem to be mocking your prospect in a "get-off-the-dime" manner, it will turn off your prospect and you'll lose a possible sale.

THE TWO-PRONGED QUESTION

While we're still on the subject of questions, let's take a brief look at the two-pronged question. This is related in its own way to the Ping-Pong question in that it allows a loophole at the end of an ordinary yes or no answer. That is, the question itself provides an alternate positive option, rather than a simple negative.

> YOU: Will you be in this afternoon? I'm in your area today and I'd like to see you.
> PROSPECT: No. I'll call you later.

Oh yeah? Sure, sure. Instead of a head-on plunge into rejection, why not try this approach?:

> YOU: I'm in the area this afternoon. Would you rather I came in to see you at two o'clock, or four?
> PROSPECT: Uh. Well, four would be better, since I'm having a late lunch.

You're in!

> YOU: Now we'll need to set up delivery on that item. When would it suit you best—the tenth or the twentieth?
> PROSPECT: Well, say the twentieth. I'll be away the tenth.

The lesson here is obvious. Never give the prospect the chance to turn you down cold. Give him two options; he'll probably settle for one.

HOW TO USE QUESTIONS FOR CONTROL

There are two important kinds of questions that are used to control the dynamics of verbal intercourse, aside from the obvious questions I have already mentioned. These two types are used in order to urge the dialogue forward, as all questions are, but at the same time they add important information to the intelligence the salesperson must always be trying to obtain.

These basic types are:

- The open-ended or leading question
- The disclosure question

By their very nature, these types of questions are used constantly in the intelligence community to elicit important information, as well as in the judicial community in order to extract the truth out of witnesses. The object of both types of question is to provide data of one kind or another. This data may be objective and specific, or subjective and abstract. In any case the data obtained can be used to put together a factual picture of whatever it is you want to know.

WHAT AN OPEN-ENDED OR LEADING QUESTION IS

Anyone who has ever switched on a television set or gone to a movie theater and seen a trial picture and viewed a courtroom in action knows what a "leading question" is. Lawyers are not supposed to "lead" their own witnesses; the truth is supposed to come to the surface naturally. If a lawyer begins leading a witness, the opposing lawyer objects, and the judge usually warns the "leading" lawyer not to "lead" any more.

ATTORNEY: On April 15, did you visit Mrs. Hendricks?

WITNESS: I did.

ATTORNEY: Was she alone?

WITNESS: There was a man with her.

ATTORNEY: What was his name?

WITNESS: Mr. Johnson.

ATTORNEY: Did they seem friendly toward one another?

WITNESS: They were quarreling.

ATTORNEY: Were they quarreling about money?

2ND ATTORNEY: Objection!

All the questions up to the key question were not leading, but the one about money was. However, in a dialogue between a salesperson and a prospect, a leading question is a perfectly permissible thing. In fact, it is a primary tool for the salesperson. In the following exchange, note how the salesperson *leads* the prospect to ask a most valuable question in turn.

YOU: Feel free to visit our entire shop. However, if you have any questions about anything, let me know. In the meantime, look around freely.

PROSPECT: Well, actually, I was looking for a special kind of copper bowl. Do you have any?

In order to elaborate a bit further, it is important to note that a leading question should be an open-ended question. Most questions in the courtroom tend to be definite yes-or-no questions:

ATTORNEY: Was the intruder wearing a green jacket? Answer yes or no!

WITNESS: No. He was wearing . . .

ATTORNEY: Confine your remarks to the question!

In court, the yes-or-no question is preferable. In business, watch what happens:

YOU: May I help you?

PROSPECT: No thanks. I'm just looking around.

"May I help you?" can be a yes-or-no question. That is, it allows the prospect to come up with a determined and final "no." Even for the prospect who might have come in to buy, you put the damper on the sale by trotting out that timeworn yes-or-no question.

> *Lesson:* Always use an open-ended or leading question that is open-ended. Never ask any question that can be construed as a yes-or-no, or you'll have a turnoff.

THE DISCLOSURE QUESTION

The disclosure question may not really be intended as such. But if the answer to any question reveals an important detail that you as a salesperson need to know, you must consider it as a disclosure question rather than anything else.

The main point here is not to allow yourself to ask a yes-or-no question, but to substitute a question that will encourage disclosure. You don't make sales by letting your prospects say "no," or, for that matter, even to *think* "no."

Here are a number of leading questions that should help you get a fair idea of how to phrase one properly:

- You're looking for quality in a product, aren't you?
- You want the warranty to cover everything that might happen, don't you?
- A reputation for integrity and honesty is important, isn't it?

And so on.

In law, there is an ancient aphorism all students at law school learn first thing: Never ask a question of a witness unless you *know* the answer yourself.

There is a very good reason for this rule of thumb. A surprise answer to a question for which the answer is unknown can throw a whole case out of balance.

In sales, the rule of thumb is just a bit different. It goes:

Never ask a prospect a question unless you are sure it can be answered without difficulty.

This presupposes a great deal of information has been given before you can get to the part with the questions in it. However, once you do get there, you can divide the questions up into open-ended questions and disclosure questions.

Ask an open-ended question that will help the prospect affirm his or her belief in what you want believed. If you tell the prospect, rather than ask, the prospect may well doubt the truth of the statement. If the prospect says it, *it's got to be true!*

Ask a disclosure question that will reveal to the prospect the benefits of the product he or she is thinking of buying. In answering the question, the prospect will reveal to you what benefits should be considered of highest priority. From this feedback, you can determine what model to try to close on.

CRASH COURSE IN ASKING QUESTIONS

There are three basic rules I like to follow whenever I use the question-and-answer technique in selling:

1. I never ask any major question until I have managed to establish some kind of rapport—a personal bond, if you will—between myself and the prospect.
2. I never give the prospect a chance to think too hard about any question, or the wrong answer may pop up.
3. I never lead people to decisions about models or features of a product until I myself have made up my mind about them.

Establishing a Personal Bond

Even though your early dialogue may be couched in questions, they should always be easy ones to answer. "Nice day, isn't it?" Until rapport is established, keep away from complex questions that involve deep thinking on some rather difficult option.

Getting a Fast Answer

You should always ask questions that can easily be answered with as little rumination as possible. The easier the concept, the quicker the answer. It is your job to tell the prospect most of the answers before you ask the questions, so that it will be easy for them to come up with the proper answer. You do this by your attitude, and in the wording of the questions.

It takes practice!

Making the Decisions for the Prospect

It is not the prospect who makes up his or her mind about the product to buy, particularly as regards specific model, color, type, or whatever. It is the salesperson, always, who decides before push comes to shove. It is the only way to operate! As the conversation goes on, you can see how the prospect is thinking by a careful watch and a thoughtful judgment of the prospect's answers to specific questions.

This is a democracy—a free country—but it is the salesperson who makes the ultimate decisions, or the sale is lost!

5

Coping Successfully with Objections

Joe Bland was one of that hardy breed, the real-estate tycoon who had started out during the Great Depression. He had gone through ups and downs of all intensities and had survived. He knew all the tricks of the trade and seemed always to be able to come up with a new one when it was needed.

It was Bland whom I like to call the Master Minimizer, that is, a man who could minimize what seemed to be a major drawback or objection to a property and transform it into a valued and desired piece of real estate.

Once he located a tract of new houses somewhere out in southern Illinois. He had been lunching with an old friend on a swing through the Midwest, and the friend told him of a group of homes in a tract that had been written off as a lost cause just the week before.

Bland was a natural masochist; he *loved* hopeless causes. He asked the friend why the houses were doomed, and the friend told him the story.

A DEVELOPER WITH THE BLIND SPOT

A builder had purchased a large tract of land on the outskirts of a middle-size town and had put up a hundred houses on it—the lots fairly ample and the quality more or less adequate to the needs of the area. These houses were bright little places, fully air-conditioned and electrically heated. Nice, easily maintained properties.

The tract had been a phenomenal success from the beginning. Lots were snapped up immediately, purchased before the houses appeared. It was a good money-maker. It was only about halfway through construction that the developer began to see a flaw in his plan. A whole strip of twelve houses along one border of the tract was unsold. No one would buy a home on the strip.

Diagnosing the Problem

For some reason the builder had neglected to compensate for the fact that there was a small airport nearby, used by local companies to ferry employees in and out to meetings and to serve commuters to Chicago and nearby areas. This airfield wasn't anything like LaGuardia in New York or O'Hare in Chicago—it was just a small field. But planes took off and landed frequently.

The twelve houses lined the side of the airport where the pilots gunned their engines for takeoff.

Now, suddenly, the developer was panicking. And by the time the tract was finished, he knew he had been right to panic. He had a good tract, but he had twelve houses that wouldn't sell. He had built close to the budget line, and he would take a blood bath for letting those houses sit.

He called the twelve houses by the only name he could think of: The Dirty Dozen.

Enter Joe Bland

Joe Bland made a deal. He told the developer he thought he could sell the houses. The developer was so happy to get someone to take a stab at selling his Dirty Dozen that he agreed to double Bland's commission on each house he could sell.

The Master Minimizer went to work. Remember that he had made his reputation in minimizing objections to property. He put an ad in the local paper, pointing out that a dozen houses in the new tract were going on sale, with a special bonus added to the package. Each house would come equipped with a large color television set, complete with VCR system and a half-dozen motion picture tapes. A kind of added incentive, of course. Nothing more.

Then Bland developed his scenario. He set up interviews with small family groups at a certain time in the morning and afternoon. When the family groups assembled, he took them through the house, showed them the main points of the place, and then brought them into the family room where the brand new television set was placed. He inserted one of the free tapes, usually a rousing musical recently on Broadway, and let it go.

The Play's the Thing

Not only the children, but the parents as well, watched the show as one of the planes would gun its engine across the field outside and wing its way into the sky. When the movie had played, Bland took the family through the house again. He made them stand at a window looking out over the airfield.

"What's that?" someone always asked.

"An airfield. The planes take off during the day. There were two that went up during the film we were watching. Actually, you get used to it."

It was obvious that no one had even *noticed.*

The Dirty Dozen Transformed

He sold all twelve of the Dirty Dozen and changed them into the Golden Dozen for himself. When he flew back home to Sacramento he had a fat bonus in his pocket.

Bland had zeroed in on the principal drawback of the location of these houses—the fact that they backed up to a noisy airport—and had *minimized* the impact of that objection in full sight and sound of his prospects. He had done it by masking the sudden interference of the noise by the noise and excitement of the free movie he had shown on his television "gift." Magic? Sure. Keep the prospect's eye on the hand that's not working the stunt.

And the buyers had to admit that the disadvantage of proximity to the airport was not so great in reality as it might have seemed in imagination.

Objections are the bane of every salesperson. Bland's manner of overcoming a staggeringly potent objection is a casebook study, if you're keeping casebooks.

> *Note:* For the average salesperson, like you and me, it's not so easy as it is for the Blands of this world. Most of the average buyer's objections are minor ones, but they do present problems just as big as Bland's. The parallel is that they can all be solved with the proper application of imagination and ingenuity.

HOW TO COPE WITH OBJECTIONS

In the chart in Chapter 4 showing the dynamics of a typical sales interview I listed "objections" as important turning points in the conversation. No sales exchange in a business discussion has ever proceeded without objections and counterclaims on each side. It is all a part of normal negotiations.

Once you have learned how to control the dynamics of verbal intercourse, you must then learn how to neutralize objections that come up during your sales presentation. Some objections are absolutely *real*. That is, there *is* a type of objection that is an insurmountable reality and can kill any sale. The good news is that this type of objection is relatively rare. The bad news is that you must be able to recognize this solid irrevocable objection and isolate it from all sorts of other excuses and wafflings that seem to be objections on the surface, but really are not.

If you fail to do so, you will allow the irrevocable objection to remain by pretending it does not exist and will have wasted your time in the end by trying to embark on a mission impossible. You'll have wasted your time flogging a dead horse, as my granddad used to say.

The unassailable objection is only one end of a rainbow of different types of objections. They fade in importance as you move through the hues of the rainbow until they become what most objections are anyway: temporary stalls, psychological mechanisms people use to put off painful decisions.

> *Translation:* A painful decision is any decision you have to make regarding the laying out of money.

I divide objections into three kinds:

- Psychological hedges
- Valid objections
- Irrevocable objections

Let's take a brief look at these first before moving on to examine each one in depth.

> PSYCHOLOGICAL HEDGES are usually temporary hesitations, or momentary acts of defiance that the prospect puts up in the ordinary course of any purchase. They can be broken down and handled with the proper skill and effort. In short, this first kind of objection is a minor one that is just an excuse not to move ahead for the time being.
>
> VALID OBJECTIONS are those objections that are more than simple stalling tactics. They may indeed prove to be important disruptions in your plan of attack. In answering a valid objection you may find that you have misqualified the prospect in some secondary way. That is, you may have mistakenly assigned the wrong model of the product or service to him or her. Valid objections can be handled without loss of the sale, but they cannot be ignored as psychological hedges can.
>
> IRREVOCABLE OBJECTIONS are the baddies. These are definitely objections that cannot be answered or fobbed off. They are, in effect, total rejections of your sales strategy. An objection of this type is a stone wall. If you try to breach it, you will only earn yourself a broken lance or a bloodied head. There is only one thing for you to do with an objection of the third kind. I'll tell you about it later.

The Real Meaning of Any Objection

The best way to think about any objection in the course of a sales exchange is to view it as an effort by the prospect to find out more about the product or service you are selling. This means that an objection is a definite indication of interest on the part of the prospect, and not a sign of disinterest. An objection does demand careful thought on your part, and must be answered carefully, clearly, and effectively. Hence all this attention to what might be considered only as a mild irritant to the person doing the selling.

It is best to consider any valid objection then as a definite asset to the salesperson. The exercise thus becomes not only ultimately to handle objections but first of all to ascertain which objections are simple psychological hedges (excuses, that is), which are valid objections, and/or which are irrevocable objections and to transform the moment into an opportunity for providing information about the product.

I like to title these three types "Objections of the First Kind (Psychological Hedges)," "Objections of the Second Kind (Valid Objections)," and "Objections of the Third Kind (Irrevocable Objections)." I'll take them up one by one, and examine how each is handled.

OBJECTIONS OF THE FIRST KIND (PSYCHOLOGICAL HEDGES)

It is in recognizing and isolating objections of the first kind that you can save yourself a great deal of time and trouble. They are not hard to recognize, nor are they difficult to deal with. Let's take a look at a list of typical excuses, for that is all such an objection is—a psychological hesitation on the way to a purchase.

- I have enough now, thanks.
- It costs too much.
- I'll think about it tomorrow (with apologies to Scarlett O'Hara).
- Business is bad, revenues are down.
- I have to discuss it with my department heads.
- I have other plans, thank you.
- I really want to think this one over.
- I'm just kind of looking around, you know.
- I really want something else.

Note that these are not real objections to any specific factual detail involving your product or your service. They are simply automatic devices grabbed out of thin air to put you off. If any one of these objections of the first kind really contributed a fact or a detail to the conversation, you could accept it as a valid objection. But none of these vapid excuses has any substance to it.

It is not really very difficult to recognize these excuses masquerading as a legitimate objections. Most of them will be quickly recognizable and isolatable. However, if you have the slightest of doubts that an objection is a real one or an empty one, you can always analyze it quickly and from your analysis draw a true conclusion about it.

The Test of Four

You put it to the Test of Four.

The Test of Four involves these four elements about the objection:

1. The customer's attitude
2. The frequency of the objection(s)
3. The timing of the objection(s)
4. A look at your customer's qualifications

1. The Customer's Attitude. I'm going into an analysis of the customer's attitude later on—physical characteristics, body language, psychological quirks—but for now you'll have to take my word for it that you can easily see from the way a prospect acts how he or she feels toward what you are saying.

If the objection is uttered in a lackadaisical tone of voice, or in a bored tone, or in an offhand manner, you will know that this is a definite objection of the first kind. It does not exist. It is an excuse, plain and simple.

Now, if the prospect comes on with a lively and spirited discourse on something he or she feels is wrong with the product or service, then you can depend on it that this objection is *not* merely an excuse. Even if it is introduced with one of the catch phrases I mentioned above, it becomes valid and viable to the degree of the prospect's *interest* as he or she delivers thought to it.

2. The Frequency of the Objection(s). An objection of the first kind is actually a smokescreen—something puffed up out of thin air to obscure direct communication between seller and buyer. The prospect is doing all he or she can in order to put obstacles in your path. Not once, not twice, but three times, and four times, and five, the prospect brings up "objections" that work like small-arms fire to pull one's interest from the main objective: a bombardment by heavy artillery.

The more of these empty excuses there are, the better you can decide that the prospect is having inner qualms and fears of being stampeded into a sale. Consider the frequency and the strength of each, and treat them accordingly. You know you are being snowballed—nibbled to death by ducks, as the saying goes.

3. The Timing of the Objection(s). If you find that your original statements and thoughts are attacked by the prospect with one objection after another—no matter what they may be—you can be sure that the prospect is simply throwing dust in your face. Most empty excuses, objections of the first kind, will be brought up during the initial phases of the verbal exchange between you.

The prospect who brings up a jumble of objections right away is obviously trying to annoy you to get rid of you. Perhaps he or she fears your ability to sell. It is obvious that the prospect does not yet know enough about the product or service to state objections. They are empty ones.

4. A Look at Your Customer's Qualifications. If you are in real doubt as to the validity of your prospect's objections—that is, if you cannot distinguish between empty excuses and real objections—there is one fallback you can rely on. Generally, you have toted your prospect's qualifications in your preliminary research. You know exactly what the prospect already has, and what he or she needs.

Thus, by examining the objections raised you can determine whether or not they are simply clouds of smoke or the real thing. If your prospect is qualified as you have analyzed him, these objections are simply empty threats to your flow of presentation.

How to Handle Objections of the First Kind

Now comes the big question. How do you handle objections of the first kind—objections that are not true objections at all, but simply hollow excuses to slow down the machinery of your sales presentation.

Ignore them.

Pretend they do not exist. (It is not a pretense; they do not in reality exist at all.)

Bypass them.

However, if you find some use in commenting on the objection, do so.

If there is no handle you can grasp to turn the objection into a selling aid, pass right on as if it were not there.

Frankly, your prospect will forget it as you continue. If he does not, then simply say, "I'll come to that later." It doesn't matter in the slightest whether you do or not.

How NOT to Handle Objections of the First Kind

Empty excuses can generate real trouble if you don't know how to handle them. Here are two definite "no-nos" for these empty objections:

- Don't argue.
- Don't attack the objection itself.

These two rules may seem to overlap, and perhaps they do. However, a quick study of them will point the truth out to you. As in this instance:

PROSPECT: Business is bad, revenues are down.

YOU: I read just this morning that things will pick up in the fall.

PROSPECT: In my business, there *is* no tomorrow.

YOU: Perhaps by using my service you will come out a winner over all your competitors!

PROSPECT: And perhaps not. The door's right over there.

The point is, the excuse about business being bad is simply an obstacle tossed in your way. By entering into a debate about it, you not only show yourself to be maneuverable, but you waste you own time as much as you waste your prospect's. You simply bat opinions back and forth—neither party winning or losing.

Second, it is pointless to attack the objection itself, because it is vapid and nonexistent in the first place. How can you argue against a puff of wind?

You can't.

So don't.

OBJECTIONS OF THE SECOND KIND (VALID OBJECTIONS)

Valid objections with substance—objections of the second kind—tend to fall into perhaps a few recognizable types. These include:

- "It's not the time to buy" objections
- Supply objections
- Service objections
- Product objections
- "Don't need the product" objections
- Price objections

The important thing to find out immediately is whether or not the "time to buy" objection falls into the category of an empty excuse, or if it is a truly real objection. The prospect may have a good reason for *not* wanting to buy immediately.

Your first move is to find out if there is a valid reason for the prospect to postpone purchase. It may well be that sales are down, that money is in short supply, that seasonal problems have arisen, that the prospect is honestly postponing the purchase for one or two very valid reasons.

By a certain amount of probing you can determine any real reason. If it turns out not to be a simple stalling technique, handle the situation the best way you can by setting a definite date to meet once again with your prospect. Never leave it up to the prospect to "call you later." You'll never hear from him or from her again. I guarantee that.

For supply, service, product, and "don't need" objections, there is a simple method for handling them. Price objections are something else again; I'll be covering that later on in a separate section. Money is a tricky business, and you'll see why it takes a great deal of concentration and a knowledge of what to promise and what not to promise.

How to Handle Objections of the Second Kind

A definite schedule for handling valid objections takes five steps. I'll be taking them up one by one after the following list:

1. Hear the objection out.
2. Pick apart the objection.
3. Answer the objection.
4. Make sure to confirm your answer.
5. Move right on to the next step.

1. Hear the Objection Out. Never fall into the trap of immediately putting up an objection to a prospect's objection. It's a temptation to move in quickly and anchor yourself to cover the objection so the prospect cannot see it anymore. Nothing will be gained by this ploy. You'll find yourself tilting at windmills, with the prospect already halfway out of the office.

If you come on too strong and too fast, you'll only arouse the prospect's suspicion that there is indeed something to the objection. You'll never be able to hide the objection from the prospect; it was he or she who thought it up in the first place.

Take your time. Listen. Take notes if you must. Hear the objection all the way through and then try to figure out how to tackle it.

2. *Pick Apart the Objection.* One valid way to tackle an objection is to elaborate on it. That is, ask your prospect to take the objection piece by piece and enumerate the details. In no way should you allow the prospect to think that you are being sarcastic by studying the objection. Never do the analysis yourself. Force the prospect to do it. It makes him think.

The main purpose here is for you to gain time as the prospect talks in order to come up with the proper answer to the objection.

There's a corollary move you can sometimes follow. If you are dealing with a dual prospect—especially a husband and wife team—you can always perform a lob. That is, bat the objection back over the net.

Hear me out. This isn't as weird as it may sound.

> THE STORY OF THE CONTENTIOUS CAR BUYERS. I was working for a car dealer at one time when I was starting out. I was a neophyte, but I was eager to learn, quick to plunge in with a supposed final solution, feisty to sell everything in sight.
>
> A husband–wife team listened to my spiel all the way through and then began probing me with questions, alternating like a tennis match. First one would come at me with something, then the other. I was getting exhausted just trying to figure out where the next pill was coming from.
>
> These questions weren't objections, really. But then came a zinger. We had pretty much decided on automatic gearshift—this was some time ago, when such a choice was still viable— and on automatic steering and braking.
>
> Suddenly the wife decided she didn't *want* automatic brakes.

I stared at her. "But it's a technological breakthrough!" I told her in astonishment.

She went right on. "I don't want automatic steering, either!"

"You *need* automatic steering—for parking ease if for no other reason!" I objected. "Besides, it makes long-distance driving that much easier."

Frankly, I was stunned. Everybody—but everybody—was opting for automatic this and automatic that. Besides, it was generally the woman of the family who preferred automatic steering and brakes—easier to use, you understand.

AND THEN EVERYTHING BLEW UP AT ONCE. While I was waiting for her answer, momentarily dumbfounded—and that's a good word for it—I heard a kind of rumble across from me. I had been so dizzy looking first at one of them and then at the other that I didn't realize the husband was beginning to come to life.

Like Vesuvius.

"What do you mean, you don't want automatic steering?" he snapped. "What do you mean, you don't want automatic brakes? We talked this over for two nights! We talked it over with the kids. Everybody wants—everybody needs—automatic brakes. How are you going to stop without them?"

"I've just decided I don't want them," she said, her chin going up.

I thought I'd better break in. "It's what everyone wants," I said in a more or less conciliatory manner. I didn't want any bloodshed in my office space. "I wouldn't *dare* sell anyone a car without either!"

There wasn't any answer. Vesuvius was rumbling again.

"We've gone over the price already, and we know what it's going to cost," the husband thundered. "I'm not going to drive a car without automatic brakes. If you want to drive it yourself, get yourself your own car! I'm not going to drive without these improvements. That's what they're for, isn't it? To improve driving?"

Blah, blah.

Actually, I got so fascinated following the ins and outs of the argument that I simply listened, right there in a kind of paid front-row seat. I had lobbed the ball back in her court, but I hadn't realized I was playing doubles! It was amusing. I had my bet on the wife, but actually the husband won. And so did I.

There is no moral here, no lesson. Just remember to lob an objection back to the lobber sometime when you're in doubt as to how to proceed. There may be other people on the court to help solve your problem for you.

3. Answer the Objection. If indeed the objection isn't an automatic excuse, and if you can't take apart the objection or let the objector take it apart, then you're going to have to move on to the third option: *You're going to have to answer the objection to the best of your ability.*

I can't help you here.

You have to do homework for this yourself.

Every product has drawbacks. It is up to you first of all to winnow out these drawbacks and dream up appropriate answers for them. The answer you produce should not be an excuse for the drawback, nor should your answer pretend the drawback does not exist. You must study it, acknowledge it, and then try to come up with some thought that will neutralize its negativity.

You can do this by simply admitting the disadvantage quickly, then going on to compare it to what you consider to be the major advantage of your product—particularly if it has a major advantage over your competition.

No matter what product or service you are trying to sell, it *is* guaranteed to possess disadvantages. You try to dream up advantages to balance out the disadvantages. Have these advantages on the tip of your tongue always. Don't bury them in your subconscious and expect them to emerge in a crisis. It doesn't happen.

You may not be able to answer the objection to the satisfaction of the prospect. If you cannot, too bad. He or she may buy the product anyway. If the prospect doesn't, just count it one against you.

4. Make Sure to Confirm Your Answer. Once you have answered the objection, don't just sit there. Make sure that the prospect *understands* the clarification. Say it out loud and wait for a response from the prospect.

> "You're sure that's an answer you can live with?"
> "That seems to solve your problem, doesn't it?"
> "Do you agree we've covered the question you raised
>   and found a way you can handle it?"
> "I'm sure that's your answer, isn't it?"

A response to any of the above will confirm the fact that the prospect understands the answer given in reference to the objection.

5. Move Right on to the Next Step. Once the objection is out of the way, move immediately on to the next point of your presentation or selling sequence.

Special Treatment: Handling the Price Objection

The most awkward and complex objection you can face is probably one of the most common: "Your price is too high."

The second, and a corollary to the first, is: "I can get it cheaper."

There are four aspects to this question that you can tackle in order to answer it. Whether or not you can ever win over your prospect is up to you—or to the prospect. The challenge of being overpriced is not something you can walk away from. The problem must be faced and discussed.

Here are the four steps you can take—either in this order or in any order you prefer.

1. Talk about the Quality of the Product. The pricing of any product or service is based on what is built into the product and contained within the service. If the best materials are used, and if the workmanship is top drawer, if design, construction, and built-in conveniences are included, and durability added to promise a long life—then the product can be shown to possess top value to any prospect.

You must have all these details organized within your mind so that you can recite them within seconds at the crucial point of your interview. As you do so, naming them in succession—materials, workmanship, design, construction, conveniences, durability—you *involve* the prospect with the superiority of these features.

2. Talk about Lower Quality Materials. If you are describing a top-quality product, you should compare it to a product that is made of cheaper materials and has a more slipshod appearance. Even if it *looks* like your product, it really is not as good, and it certainly doesn't perform as well.

Poor quality will always be there to remind you of the inferior nature of the product; good quality will give you long-lasting service and be a joy to behold. If you buy a cheap product, you will pay for it in the long run with less serviceable efficiency.

3. Talk about the Negative Aspects of Cheapness. There are plenty of horror stories around about cheap goods. You should keep a fund of them on hand in order to balance them against the story of buyers with *good* products. If you are handling a quality product—and you probably are if you get complaints about cost—you will be able to point out that there is a built-in advantage to a good product, in that it usually does not attract disasters the way a cheap product does.

4. Play on the Prospect's Pride. Now is the time for you to turn to the prospect's pride. By purchasing a quality item, he or she should feel good about it. Possessing a quality item of any kind is a plus factor to anyone. In fact, it raises the prospect's prestige value in the eyes of others.

Nobody brags about owning a cheap piece of junk. High-priced items build prestige for their owners. The quality of the item possessed in a way seeps out and enters the image of the owner. Thus the individual with a high-priced item becomes just a little bit better in the eyes of those who behold him or her than before. A little bit of the clout of any expensive item rubs off on its owner.

Essentially, that's the reason that diamonds are a girl's best friend.

OBJECTIONS OF THE THIRD KIND (IRREVOCABLE OBJECTIONS)

Minor objections may be defense mechanisms; major objections may prove to be stepping stones to larger products; but a true objection in the sense of a stumbling block to a sale can prove a disaster to the seller.

It is my studied opinion that almost all objections fall into categories one and two. However, there are times when everything you have built up in your sales pitch falls apart. Sometimes no one knows the reason for it. Other times there are personality clashes between salesperson and prospect.

Generally speaking, a true objection of the third kind is a sudden stop in the conversation. The prospect abruptly changes persona right in front of you. If it's a man, he folds his arms across his chest and frowns. If it's a woman, she may stiffen in the chair and stare at you coldly.

At that point, no matter what your prospect or prospects say, it's all over.

Identifying an Objection of the Third Kind

I was once asked to describe an objection of the third kind, and I was at a loss to put it into words. Frankly, it's an objection that is not a psychological hedge or a valid objection. It's something that comes between you and the prospect and ruins the sale.

I was once selling a washing machine to a woman. She was quite friendly, and listened to all my statements about the advantages and benefits of the machine. I thought I had her hooked. But quite suddenly in the middle of the last five minutes of my spiel, she stood up, took a turn around the room, and then came over and stared right at me.

"You have funny piggy little eyes. Do you know that?"

My mouth dropped open.

"I don't want any machine you'd sell me." And she turned around and walked out.

What to do with an objection of the third kind?

A true objection of the third kind is a fatal blow to any hopes of a sale. If you do encounter such an objection, analyze it, study it, and when you determine it is truly a block, turn away from the sale and forget it.

It's as simple as that.

Take a lesson from a professional poker player. A good poker player always knows when he has drawn a poor hand. He simply folds and throws in his cards when he faces a losing play. You will notice that he differs from the average or cheapskate card player. The cheapskate doesn't understand the game enough to realize when he has had it. He stays in and wins one, and loses one. Generally he stays in too long and loses everything before the night is out.

Golden rule: Objections of the third kind are fatal. If you run across one and analyze it as such, throw your shoulders back, turn around, and walk away—fast. But happily, knowing that you've avoided a total disaster.

6

Getting to the Heart of the Prospect

The theater lights dim on *Music Man*. One man is visible onstage. There is a sense of menace in the air, in spite of the fact that this is a joyous and feisty musical comedy. A hush spreads over the audience. In the lights an actor—remarkably similar in appearance to the late Robert Preston—looks out over the theater and begins his musical sermon:

"Ya got Trouble, my friends, right here in River City!"

River City, Iowa, that is—Meredith Willson's fictional name for Mason City, Iowa, where he was born.

"Trouble, with a capital T, and that rhymes with P, and that stands for *Pool!*"

90

IDLE HANDS ARE THE DEVIL'S WORKSHOP

Study the lyrics of that sermon for a moment. Remember it's a sermon delivered by a man who has come to town sporting the name of Professor Harold Hill, an authority on matters of musicology. The truth is that deep down, in the real world, Hill is a salesman—or "salesperson" in the jargon of the post-NOW years.

The *trouble* in River City involves the younger generation, according to Professor Hill—growing up all unwary and innocent, but threatened by unseen dangers, including the use of slang words like "swell!" and "so's your old man!" and "ragtime!" And jokes from *Cap'n Billy's Whiz Bang!* The youngsters are taking the first step on the road to DEGRADATION! *Evil* lurks out there!

That's the Professor's opening gambit.

Let's Form a Band and March!

There's more: the middle game and the end game. After the menace is exposed by the Professor, and he gets the attention of the good people in River City, he suddenly pops the proper solution to them. Why not get the kids interested in something *important?* Like—say, hey!—music! Why not get all the kids musical instruments to practice on, make the small-fry into musicians, and work them in together to make—music?!

That's Professor Harold Hill's middle game.

Why not form a kids' band? Why not *buy* musical instruments so that everyone in River City can be musically capable? Why not *order* those instruments from Chicago, or New York, or somewhere important—and get the best! Why not form the greatest band in the—in the Territory?

Sold! That's the end game. That's the successful closing. And the end result of Professor Hill's mission in River City is the exultation felt by the citizens and the children of the town in the final formation of their kids' band—complete with its amazing seventy-six trombones.

In fact, Professor Hill has been so successful in initiating this marvelous kids' band that in the end he decides to stay in River City where he lives happily ever after!

The Sermon on the River

For the moment let's study the "sermon" delivered by Professor Harold Hill. Actually, it is a rousing sales pitch in the disguise of a sociological treatise on good and evil. But it is a splendid elaboration of one of the key elements in any well-prepared sales proposal.

The points in the sermon literally *create* a need for a product—in this case, musical instruments—where the need for them has previously barely existed. Oh, of course, most people in River City knew what musical instruments were, but they knew it was not necessary for every person to have one.

The sermon *creates a need for* musical instruments, and, by the end of Professor Hill's discourse, it *sells* that idea to the town, which now *needs* musical instruments it never before considered important for day-to-day living.

The beauty of it is that no one realizes the sermon is a sales pitch; everyone reacts according to messages from his or her psyche (for "psyche" read "heart" or "soul").

Creating a NEED in the Consumer

Professor Harold Hill has cleverly transferred the non-need of a semiluxury item—at least a product of dubious vital necessity—to a *needed* product. To a product that, according to Professor Hill, is needed to save the city from the depredations of sin.

Yes, it's a story. Yes, it's a comedy. Yes, it's unbelievable in the long run. But while you're in the theater, it works.

And the reason it works is that Professor Harold Hill (manipulated like a puppet by his creator Meredith Willson) is a born salesperson who knows how to reach the hearts of his prospects.

I have pointed out that "psyche" refers either to "heart" or "soul." It is the *psyche* that Hill manipulates. He manipulates it by appealing to certain facets of the personality of the prospects he is anxious to sell. *Psyche* is an old Greek word that refers to the soul; today we use the word in derivatives that refer not to the soul, but to the inner mechanisms of the persona. It is psychology that Hill is using— psychology to play on certain elements of the human psyche. Elements that are *motivators*.

HOW TO PLUG INTO THE PSYCHE

Let's look at a few of these motivators.

Obviously the first and foremost facet of the psyche that Professor Hill is interested in is *fear*. It is the fear of evil that becomes his target; he wants to arouse that fear in those who listen to his spiel.

But he is also arousing another important psychological emotion simultaneously: *pride*. It is the end result of purchasing the instruments that is the point of the sermon; and if you do buy band instruments, you'll be *proud* of the band that will have—as it would have in the end—seventy-six trombones!

Two basic emotions here—fear and pride—are what makes the sales appeal of Professor Hill work. But there are concomitant emotions as well that Professor Hill reaches.

He is, actually, quite clever in appealing to the *vanity* of every citizen of River City. And, along with vanity, he is working on a companion feature of the psyche: *envy*. Won't others *envy* River City with its marvelous marching band?

In turn a great many other psychological benefits will accrue to the people of River City when they have formed their grand band.

Won't they find *pleasure* in listening to the music the

band makes? Won't they thrill to the *comfort* this gives them? Won't they feel that the *status* of the town will be raised higher than anyone ever expected? Won't they feel *power* in realizing that River City is better than any other place in Iowa?

The Trick of Appealing to the Emotions

The important point to note here is that at least eight strong, recognizable motivators have been stirred by Hill's sales pitch. Let's face it, the sermon is a fraud; it is strictly a sales pitch to get the citizens of River City to open up their wallets and shell out money.

With a little further exploration I am sure we could find other paralleling motivators aroused as well: a sense of *mission,* for example; the *covetousness* of owning beautiful instruments; the *security* of the children; the possibility of even a kind of *lustful* joy in hearing the rousing music (although that's stretching it just a bit).

Professor Hill's lesson is actually not a lesson at all. My lesson, regarding Hill's sermon, is the real lesson. The lesson is to teach you how to get to the heart of the prospect. And the way to get to the heart of the prospect is through his or her *psyche.*

You have to know how to get to the psyche, however. There is a right way as well as a wrong way. You may as well get it right if you try it. Otherwise you are wasting your time.

A DOZEN WAYS TO TURN A PROSPECT ON

I'm going to winnow out the twelve emotions mentioned above for further study—study in how to utilize approaches to them correctly *and* incorrectly.

Here, then, is a list. (*Note:* It is only a partial list, but appropriate for this specific example.)

1. Fear
2. Pride
3. Status
4. Vanity
5. Covetousness
6. Lust
7. Pleasure
8. Envy
9. Power
10. Comfort
11. Mission
12. Security

You may note that the list *reminds* you of something else—perhaps another well-known list. And, you can be sure, it *does* resemble the famous list of Medieval theology's Seven Deadly Sins, which are:

1. Anger
2. Covetousness
3. Envy
4. Gluttony
5. Lust
6. Pride
7. Sloth

See? Envy, pride, covetousness, and lust are on both lists. Gluttony and the lust for power are almost the same thing. The similarities are mind-boggling.

I'm bringing up the similarity not to denigrate the use of appeal to these motivators, but to point out how common they are and how much they affect every one of us throughout our lives. Of these, naturally, the most powerful of all is the simple psychological manifestation of *fear*.

WHAT *FEAR* MEANS TO THE SALESPERSON

Riding all our backs throughout our lifetimes is that old demon fear.

- Fear of death
- Fear of starvation
- Fear of drowning
- Fear of poverty
- Fear of rejection
- Fear of what tomorrow will bring
- Fear of fear itself!

Although fear is a negative emotion, it is certainly a viable element in anyone's psyche. For that reason it is probably the easiest motivator to reach and the one that produces the most powerful responses in the person in whom it is aroused.

A salesperson who peddles insurance always pretends *not* to be selling an antidote to fear; I say, ha ha. Fear *is* the basis of all insurance. Yet a good salesperson never draws attention to this basic emotion, because the average prospect's reaction to mention of it tends to be a disturbing one and becomes a negative issue if brought forward. It is an element in the psyche that is best left on the back burner, although it is never forgotten by the seller or the buyer.

... So Keep It Out of Sight

Nevertheless, the salesperson should always be aware of the drive of fear in the sales interview of any product or service. In expounding on any safety feature of a product like an automobile, the idea of fear of death hovers over the discussion like a rain cloud over the head of Charlie Brown.

Always deal with such features in a positive way. The negative is there, implicit, underground, submerged deep in the psyche. Let it stay there. Never forget, however, that it *is* there, and what a powerful motivating force it can be in the final closing moments of any sale.

WHAT *PRIDE* MEANS TO THE SALESPERSON

The fact that pride is one of the Seven Deadly Sins came somewhat as a shock to me when I was growing up. I always looked on the idea of "being proud" as something that reflected highly on me.

"I'm proud of you, son," my mother said, in those odd times when I might bring home an A on my report card.

"I'm proud of you," my father said to back up my mother's good feeling.

Pride is just that: a *good* feeling. You take pride in a job well done.

The question that always bothered me was this: why was pride one of the Seven Deadly Sins?

. . . And Why to Bury It Deep

There is, of course, a kind of flaunting pride that is bothersome to people. Someone who possesses a lot, who spends big, and who makes everyone around him or her grovel in inferiority, is deliberately arousing everyone's envy. It is obvious that the Bible is viewing pride as false pride of this kind when it says in Proverbs 16:19:

Better *it is to be* of an humble spirit with the lowly, than to divide the spoil with the proud.

In the paragraph preceding it is the more famous line:

Pride *goeth* before destruction, and a haughty spirit before a fall.

That is the "bad" kind of pride, the false, flaunting pride that grates on one.

The reality of pride exists deep within the psyche of everyone. It is there to be touched and brought alive, if you have the proper training to do it. In a difficult sales situation, this motivator is a formidable ally for you to bring into life. Have it ready for use when you need it!

WHAT *STATUS* MEANS TO A SALESPERSON

It might strike you as odd that the Bible does not discuss "status." The word does not even appear. A little further thought may bring out the obvious fact that personal status was preordained in the ancient world. A person was born a king, a peasant, or a slave. That became his position in life forever.

America is the first total experiment in democracy, stripped completely of the trappings of privilege (as in Britain, and as in ancient Greece with its slaves). In a democracy, status is determined by the individual, by his or her circumstances, by his or her abilities, by the timing of his or her efforts, by the direction in which he or she is going, and a number of other relevant variables.

The Way Status Affects Us

Although our reasoning is fallacious, we look on a person's status as a picture of his or her abilities, endurance, and talents. Thus status is extremely important to everyone who exists in our society. Somehow it is seen as a stamp of approval more or less arrived at by a general view of a person's character and potentialities. (I hedge this by pointing out that status is an *artificial* stamp of approval, having in many cases little to do with the truth of a person's worth.)

Because a democracy is a free-wheeling social organization of people in which one makes his or her way to the top as quickly and as cleanly as possible, status becomes a definite measure of one's upward mobility. A high status implies superiority. A low status implies inferiority. It is that simple. Other factors are not considered at all; they *should* be. Life, however, is not always as it *should* be.

The Driving Force Within Us

High status is a reward in itself. Everyone else looks up to the high achiever—at least at someone whose high achievement has awarded him or her a high status. Many high achievers are crushed in the race to the top and fall back to the bottom. Thus status in America (in any democracy) is a definite sign of success, a kind of approval rating given one by his or her peers.

There burns within each of us the feeling that our status is always under challenge; that someone else is trying to move past us; that those above us scorn us because we are trying to arrive at their level. In many people—I'll take a chance and say in *most* people—status is a burning and driving force.

A good salesperson knows this. An intelligent salesperson *uses* this force as much as possible to unlock the power within to drive the prospect toward the product or service being offered, making it a positive potential to elevate the prospect's status.

WHAT *VANITY* MEANS TO A SALESPERSON

Vanity of vanities, saith the Preacher, vanity of vanities; all *is* vanity.

The Preacher referred to in this line from Ecclesiastes is King Solomon, whose wisdom has extended long past his time on earth. Some researchers claim it was written some time after the death of Solomon, but it is generally attributed in the public mind to Solomon's wisdom.

The theme of the sermon is that, since all is vanity, that is, empty pleasure and fun and games, you should enjoy life while you live it because death is always waiting to put an end to it.

The word *vanity* surfaces occasionally in odd places:

- A woman's "vanity" is a makeup kit.
- Vanity Fair in literature was a fair held by empty-minded people intent only on their own pleasure. (Suggested Reading: John Bunyan's *Pilgrim's Progress.*)
- A vanity plate is a license plate with the car owner's name on it.
- A vanity press is a publishing house that charges the author to print his book.

Vanity, vanity—a great deal of life is vanity. Particularly the vanity that is satisfied when one displays his or her status as highly and as marvelously as possible.

Mainlining the Vein of the Vain

This pool of emotion lies within each of us, waiting to be tapped whenever it can be. No salesperson worthy of his or her salt ever forgets that all-important fact.

The salesperson trying to sell a flowery dress to an upper-middle-class woman of enormous girth stands back, clasps her hands, and widens her eyes so they sparkle:

"Oh, it's you, my dear! It's *you.*"

Vanity springs up within the prospect. It blooms. She buys the dress, which settles on her like a bedouin's tent in a sandstorm.

Again, like fear and like status, vanity is a powerful and compelling emotional motivator in selling products or services. After all, it is *difficult* to be noticed; it is almost impossible to look *right.* Whatever a product or a service can do to make someone look *good* can be made to be much more appealing to the vanity of the prospect.

Tom Wolfe was quite aware of the power of vanity when he came to title his 1988 best-seller: *The Bonfire of the Vanities.*

As a salesperson, make sure you never lose sight of it or forget about it.

WHAT *COVETOUSNESS* MEANS TO A SALESPERSON

Covetousness is a word that has gone out of fashion over the years. A lot of people don't even bother to learn what it means. It means *cupidity*, which in turn has nothing to do with Cupid, although you'd be surprised at how many people of normal education think it does have a connection with naked angels that run around with bows and arrows.

In fact, covetousness/cupidity comes from the Latin *cupiditas*, and refers to that inner feeling of *need* for things that everyone gets at one time or another. Covetousness has nothing to do with wealth or with poverty. Poor people suffer from covetousness as well as rich.

For the rich, covetousness causes even more suffering than for the poor. Once the miser has his gold coins, he counts them again and again, gloating over his possessions. He wants to keep counting them, and thus is unable to purchase any worldly goods; to do so would deprive him of the very coins that prove his worth.

He wants his coins and he wants what they will buy *at the same time.*

Covetousness is a driving force in any human being, in any prospect. The trick is to be able to seize on it at the proper moment.

The LOOK of Covetousness

I never thought about my own covetousness much until a good friend spotted it and told me about it. You know already that my favorite game is chess and you know how much emphasis I put on a good chess game.

About a year ago I found an ivory chess set in a shop window down near my New York apartment. It was a simply marvelous thing, hand-carved out of ivory, with special gonfalons for the knights, and flowing robes for the bishops, full regalia for the king and the queen. I don't know how they managed to blacken the ivory, but the black pieces were every bit as exciting as the white ones.

I'd go by that window and stare in at the thing, memorizing the look of the pieces. I determined not to buy it. I wasn't going to be a fool. My chess partner was always miles away from me. It was not for me. Repeat: not.

Who Bought My Chess Set?

An old friend was walking with me along the street one night after dinner on the way to my place when I noticed that the shop owner had shifted the chess set out of the window. I was brokenhearted. It had been sold! I no longer had a chance to look at that marvelous ivory chess set!

I was so concerned that I turned and walked into the store, my companion following me with a puzzled smile on her face. I confronted the shop owner and demanded to know who had bought the chess set that had been in the window for months.

He shrugged and pointed to one of the counters. I turned and stared. The set was assembled on the board inside the glass counter. He had not sold it all. He had simply taken it out of the window to put something out there that seemed to him to have more sales value.

I continued staring at my chess set.

Finally I turned and walked out of the shop without saying anything.

"You Should SEE Yourself!"

My friend started to chuckle as soon as we had gotten out of sight of the shop. I was annoyed. I stopped and turned on her.

"What are you laughing about? What's so funny?"

"If you could *see* the look on your face!" she giggled, holding her hand over her mouth. "If you could *see* yourself!"

I grew even more irritated. "What do you mean *see* myself?"

"But it's so obvious!" And she went into another long spell of laughing.

I stomped on down the sidewalk. She caught up with me. "Wait!"

"Forget it! I don't see the joke!"

"*You're* the joke," she told me, finally controlling her mirth. "The *look* on your face! It was as if you were looking at the Empress of India diamond, of the Queen of England's jewels. You were gloating! *Gloating!*"

"Gloating?" I repeated. "Over what?"

"You *wanted* that set! You would *die* to get it! Why don't you buy it?"

I had no answer.

"It *glowed* out of you," she told me later. "You *lusted* for that set—more than you ever lusted for any human being, I'm sure." She giggled again.

A Little Lust, a Little Desire . . .

That's how I got my ivory chess set. She gave it to me for Christmas. And I took the tip and learned to look for that little flash of covetousness in my next prospect. It doesn't surface every time. But when you're dealing with certain products that have the value of beauty among their features, you sometimes can see it.

It's a gleam in the eye. It's a loose-lipped stare. It's total concentration on the beloved object. Look for it. You can *see* it, just as my friend did. When you see it, move in for the kill.

You're on the verge of closing.

WHAT *LUST* MEANS TO A SALESPERSON

One of the most ridiculous fantasies in advertising or in salesmanship is to assume that sex appeal is an overused and overstated method of selling products and services. Of course, it's usually used in such a blatant fashion that it is laugh-provoking, rather than sales-stimulating.

A pair of shock absorbers appears in the middle of a picture, gleaming and utilitarian as always, but the photographer has managed to pose a young woman in a very revealing bathing suit right next to it, or directly behind it. What is this—a joke?

The joke's on you, really.

Machine-shop calendars have featured beautiful nudes in sexy poses for most of the twentieth century.

Even blue jeans are marched about on svelte-looking blondes and brunettes—a perfect example of a clod product promoted in a chic setting.

Women's liberation has definitely changed the attitude of the public toward the sexes. Women get the same jobs as men now. They're paid as much, sometimes. There is the unisex haircut offered in barber shops. Barber shops, not beauty shops!

Women run footraces with men. Women compete in athletics—on baseball teams, on basketball teams, even in boxing and wrestling matches.

With everyone equal, how can you sell using sex appeal?

Forget all about the nondifferentiation of the sexes. The difference is still there. Use it when you can!

WHAT *PLEASURE* MEANS TO A SALESPERSON

A couple of years ago one of the automobile companies got together a marvelous little scenario. The storyboard of the commercial began with a man driving up in a brand-new sporty-looking car. He climbs out of the car, looks up on the front porch of a large, comfortable, middle-America type of house—all clapboards and shuttered windows.

"Nobody drives this but me!" he announces firmly. "Understood?"

A family group of three generations look on, each nodding the head in agreement. There's the son, the daughter, the wife, the wife's sister, and grandma. Grandma is knitting.

Next we see the car cutting through the roadways, the fields, the tree-lined highways, with the radio going full blast, playing a catchy rendition of "La Bamba."

The car slams to a stop in front of the house.

The next thing we see is the man stalking down the steps of the front porch and climbing into the car. He looks down at the speedometer.

"Who's been using my car?" he bellows out.

The same family group is on the porch once more. Nobody admits to anything. The kids shake their heads. The wife and sister shrug. Grandma is knitting.

He drives off.

We close in on grandma, who is humming, under her breath, the catchy beat of "La Bamba" that was blasting out of the gallivanting car.

The message is plain. You can *feel* it. Driving that car is *fun*. It's a gasser, as Sinatra might have said twenty years ago. All in all, it's sporty and it's youthful and it keeps you alive, no matter how old in years you are.

Why, even grandma—

It's a neat little package of salesmanship.

Is Pleasure Sinful?

Pay no attention to the idea that people think of pleasure as something sinful. Oh, sure, that's been one of the main tenets of Puritanism. The idea is to suffer to get to Heaven. Perhaps the belief was true three hundred or so years ago in this country, but don't try to tell me it's still fashionable.

Even Lord Byron knew the truth almost two hundred

years ago, when he wrote that epic poem titled *Don Juan*, about the Great Lover. Here's the way he put it:

Pleasure's a sin, and sometimes sin's a pleasure.

You don't need to *remind* people of that; they know it as well as you do. Use the truth in your salesmanship. It may well reinforce a sagging sales pitch.

WHAT *ENVY* MEANS TO A SALESPERSON

I already pointed out that envy is one of the Seven Deadly Sins. If the world were perfect and if people acted unlike the way people do, then there would be no such thing as envy.

Unfortunately, people do not act the way they should, and envy is a motivating factor in all sorts of human ills. It is also a buried element in anyone's personality. The damnedest things cause people to envy others.

- *Beauty.* That's probably a natural thing to envy.
- *Money.* Our society's *made* that a source of envy.
- *Power.* That's a source of clout that anyone can envy in another person.
- *Possessions.* That's where your salesmanship comes in.

The idea of owning something of superior quality, craftsmanship, and beauty is not complete in itself. It is the idea that ownership of something of superior quality raises envy in others who do not have it that stimulates a *need* in a buyer.

As long ago as the time when Elizabeth I was Queen of England, Sir Francis Bacon, a member of the court and friend of Essex, was aware of the nature of envy. In his magnum opus *De Augmentia Scientarum* (1623), he wrote:

Envy never makes holiday.

John Gay, the author of the *Beggar's Opera*—modernized and still popular as the *Three-Penny Opera*—put envy into focus this way:

Envy's a sharper spur than pay.

You won't be able to base your whole sales pitch on envy, but you can always reinforce it by surreptitiously calling it up in your prospect. It's easy to make your prospect *see* the envy in the eyes of those looking at his new product; that alone will make him sign his name on the dotted line.

WHAT *POWER* MEANS TO A SALESPERSON

Even though the trendy term for the old-fashioned concept of power—as in the Bible's phrase, "the power and the glory forever"—is "clout," I choose to use the more acceptable and historic one. Both power and clout mean absolutely the same thing.

Clout is something you either have or you do not have. Clout walks in the room with you. Clout emanates from you, pervades the atmosphere about you, circulates into the auras of all those near you. It is a magnetic field; people *feel* it when you are near them. Clout gets you ringside seats at *the* event of the season. Clout gets you box seats at the Superbowl. Clout manages to procure that favorite table at the crowded Four Seasons in New York.

Power—your ability to wield it and control it—affords you clout. Without access to power, you cannot wield clout. Without power you do not get named within the first five spots of Fortune's Five Hundred Most Important Businesspersons in Industry.

And so when a salesperson perceives someone who lusts for power, he or she knows exactly what to do: appeal to that inner *need*.

Where Does Power Come from?

Why do you think there is such a thing as a "power" breakfast, a "power" lunch, a "power" dinner? To make each event important, to give it clout, to make it something no one will ever forget.

There is a shortcut you can take if you cannot find the proper key to open up your prospect to the concept of power. It exists in an understanding of the phrase: "Money is power."

He who has money has power. Therefore, money is a key factor in power. By arousing the concept of money and wealth in the prospect, you've come one step nearer to arousing your prospect's need for power.

Power tends to corrupt and absolute power corrupts absolutely.

That is from Sir J. E. E. Dalberg, the First Baron Acton.

But remember it. The idea of power is so strong that it becomes a potent tool in the hands of someone who wants to persuade that person to do something.

WHAT *COMFORT* MEANS TO A SALESPERSON

The concept of comfort is another important motivator lurking in the psyche and waiting for some imaginative salesperson to stimulate.

"Comfort me with apples," Solomon sang in the Bible, "for I am sick of love." The idea of comfort in ancient times was obviously on a par with the idea of love (sex)—*both* important considerations no matter how you look at it.

A more cynical Samuel Butler wrote in typical Butler fashion in the nineteenth century:

It costs a lot of money to die comfortably.

Following Butler's lead, the twentieth-century use of the word "comfortable" has come to be a sly way of saying "wealthy," or—that crudity of crudities—"rich."

King John, who had been poisoned apparently by someone traitorous to the English cause, calls on those around him in Shakespeare's chronicle:

> I do not ask you much:
> I beg cold comfort; and you are so strait
> And so ingrateful you deny me that.

Cold comfort. A far cry from what we call "solid comfort."

Solid Comfort Today

The picture of "solid comfort" that springs to mind today is that of a man in leisure clothes lying in a hammock slung between two trees, holding a glass of some kind of sparkling beverage in his hand, and grinning up at the birds chirping in the trees against a cloudless sky of blue.

That's the image to which you should play as a salesperson. It is our picture of solid comfort. If you can inspire thoughts of such a scene in the mind of your prospect, you have half the battle of selling won.

It's interesting to note that this vision of comfort parallels that of "sloth," that old-fashioned word that could be translated today into "laziness," or, more mildly, "leisure." And "sloth," as we have seen, is one of the Medieval Ages' Seven Deadly Sins.

Play to it—it lurks in all of us—and win!

WHAT *MISSION* MEANS TO A SALESPERSON

In spite of an incredible lack of visibility, there is in almost everyone today some submerged sense of mission that burns at a low but inextinguishable level. This mission is a goal of some kind that exists in one's psyche.

For some, the mission is to provide shelter for the homeless; that is generally considered to be a *political* mission.

For others, the mission is to raise the standards of education in America; that is generally considered to be a *sociological* mission—and a worthy one indeed.

For most of us, our *sense of mission* is somewhat called down from these lofty ones.

- To keep the lawn in shape every weekend
- To have the family boat in the water during the sailing months
- To get a Grade A dinner on the table each evening

Let's skip back to Professor Harold Hill. Professor Hill *created* a mission in the minds of the citizens of River City. He made them *want* River City to have the greatest kids' band in the midwest. By the time he was through his spiel, he had made that mission the foremost need in the minds of everyone who heard him.

How to Tap a Sense of Mission

It is difficult to discover the secret mission of another person, unless you are closely enough attuned to that person's psychological makeup to spot clues as to its shape and size. Usually these seep out in basically innocuous remarks about day-to-day events. From these a good detective can put together a vision of what *mission* is motivating the other person.

Mission is not a *key* concept in selling a prospect. But if you can spot it—or create it, as Professor Hill did—then you have a powerful motivator you can use in persuading the prospect to buy.

The guiding principle here is simply to keep your eyes and ears open for any indication of a burning inner mission in your prospect. Then, when you've identified it—use it!

WHAT *SECURITY* MEANS TO A SALESPERSON

Franklin D. Roosevelt was perplexed and concerned. He had been in the Oval Office in Washington for only a few months, and he knew he had to do *something* about all the people who were penniless and with no prospect of jobs.

The British had solved the problem by implementing a "dole," a simple handout of money to each out-of-work person by a concerned government.

F.D.R. was a pragmatist, but he was also sensitive to the various feelings of the labor class in America. He knew that he would be working against—not with—the pride of the average person if he instituted a dole like the one in England.

He knew specifically that an American wanted to work for his money—not stand in line and receive it like a beggar. It was matter of bitter *pride.*

Roosevelt was a salesperson, as well as a politician. He knew he had to *sell* the idea of the dole he was going to use— sell it to the prospect, that is, the American people.

He disguised it. To disguise it, he reached for another one of the emotional motivators we have been discussing and used it.

That motivator was "security."

- Security meant being safe at night in your own home.
- Security meant being able to feed your family.
- Security meant being able to clothe your family, and house them as well.
- Security meant feeling good about your present and your future.

Roosevelt reshuffled the dole, created a reason for it, and in addition molded it into a pseudo-pension plan under- written by the federal government, and called it "social security." The words became a term indelibly engraved on the mind of the American people. It is still there today. The key word is "security."

He knew where to arouse feelings of response in the

average person. He knew that he could establish in his "fellow Americans" a feeling of rightness and integrity in the use of the term "social security" to hide the fact that this new concept was in actuality a simple dole handed out in the depths of the Great Depression to people who had lost their jobs and their dignity and had no money to live on.

It worked.

The Number One politician of the century had become the Number One salesperson.

By such quantum leaps of the imagination, the mediocre salesperson can become the Number One salesperson. In short, the mediocre salesperson becomes Number One by learning how to get to the *heart* of the prospect. That's where the motivators are; that's where the wellsprings of desire and need are.

The Turning Point: When to Close

"What is truth?" said jesting Pilate; and would not stay for an answer.

In the epigraph statement above, Francis Bacon was referring to Pontius Pilate's answer to Jesus Christ, who stood before him claiming to be the King of the Jews. "To this end was I born," Jesus had told Pilate, "and for this cause came I into the world, that I should bear witness to the truth. Every one that is of the truth heareth my voice."

And so Pontius Pilate gave the answer above just before he sent Jesus to be crucified.

THE DIFFICULTY WITH TRUTH

Modern society finds it every bit as difficult to determine the truth as ancient society did. Modern science, which has unlocked many secrets of the universe, has almost succeeded in developing a machine that can determine truth, or at least its close approximation, in the polygraph. In common parlance, reversing the point of view from truth to prevarication, we perversely call the "truth machine" a "lie detector."

Although vilified by attorneys, judges, and some police officials, the polygraph is the nearest thing modern man has for determining the truth or falsehood of an individual's statement. It must be admitted that its accuracy is still in doubt in many cases. But it has been known to detect lies and to determine truths to a certain degree.

Essentially, the polygraph ("poly" = many; "graph" = picture) measures scientifically the fluctuations of a number of different physiological variables: blood pressure, heartbeat, perspiration, respiration, and some body movements. The machine was developed first by John A. Larson in 1921, and later refined by Allen Bell with the addition of psychological stress evaluations.

WHAT YOU SEES IS NOT NECESSARILY WHAT YOU GETS

Philosophers and psychologists have known for centuries that there is no philosophical imperative that forces an individual to tell the truth. At the same time, is has been noted that the mind that determines the lie is not entirely disassociated from the human physiology attached to it.

For the moment take yourself back to your youth. You were instructed from birth never to tell a lie. In spite of that, you may have fibbed to your peers occasionally. Now you are in a situation in which you are in deep trouble. To take the most common occurrence of all, you have just stolen a cookie out of the cookie jar, defying your mother's specific injunctions *not* to. And she has caught you.

"Did you take a cookie out of that jar?" she asks you.

Theoretically you should be able to look your mother right in the eye and calmly tell her that you did not. You should be able to say "no" coolly and deliberately.

Perhaps you can do so—but what is happening in the rest of your persona?

Plenty! Witness:

- Your pulse is racing.
- Your heart is crowding into your throat.
- Perspiration is bursting out on your skin.
- Your scalp is crawling.
- Your palms are hot and moist.
- There is a crimson glow seeping up into your face.
- Your eyes are hot and teary.
- You have developed all kinds of bodily tics.

These indications are only a part of the physiological pattern. But they are enough to point out the truth. The hard fact is that the human psyche—the individual you—is programmed from birth to *tell the truth*.

Body Language Doesn't Lie

Thus, when you tell a lie, your body—your physiological system—revolts against the idea of prevarication. Your body language counteracts the language of your tongue. And so when you tell your mother that no, you did not take the cookie (that you *did* take), your body betrays you. And she determines the truth by watching you and what your body does, not by listening to the words you say.

This fact of life is the basis of the polygraph's measurements. The machine determines the fluctuations of the various physiological measurements already mentioned. The pictures, in the form of graphs, of pulsations hum along at a regular rate when your language is in sync with the truth; but when your language is in sync with the truth; but when your language deviates from the truth, your body graphs fluctuate dramatically—high peaks, thick surges, etc.

Logging the Internal Struggle Between Mind and Body

By measuring all these physiological deviations while conversing with you, the polygraph operator can check back to find out which answers occur under normal physiological circumstances, and which answers cause abnormal fluctuations—that is, when you lie.

Long before the polygraph came into being, human beings understood the internal war between the mind and the body—between the truth and the voice. The body itself tended to *cringe* at certain untruths. Thus body language has been obvious for centuries, but it has only been put to use in the very recent past.

In my first book, *The First Five Minutes*, I made a point of discussing the elements of body language. I told you how to get your act together, that is, to make sure your body language reflected your mind's language. I told you to underline your verbal statements with corresponding body language.

Now I'm going to turn that concept inside out and talk about using body language not to further your own purposes, but to determine the true reactions in the person with whom you are holding conversation—probably trying to sell a product, a service, or even yourself.

THE ART OF READING PEOPLE

To put it in another way, I'm going to talk to you about your abilities as a drama critic, the person who watches a play and notes that the actor playing the role isn't getting into the part, doesn't say his lines right, and has been miscast for the role.

The reason I am going to talk about in-depth analysis of another person's persona—particularly if it is conflicted—is that reading your prospect is a crucial factor in the final determination of the absolutely correct time at which to start your closing moves in an interview.

Let's create an imaginative situation. You've qualified your prospect—in this scenario your prospect is a man—you've made your initial moves to meet him and analyze him, you've gained a good idea of where he is coming from and what he needs, you've given him a good presentation or proposal of your product or service, and you're approaching what you hope to be the turning point in the discussion.

Now for a brief digression about the so-called turning point. This is the point in any business, job, or sales interview when everything has been discussed and ironed out, when there are no more objections to be answered or neutralized, when everything seems to hang in the balance.

It is at this moment that you must try to bring about a closing. That is, it is at this moment that you embark on what I am calling The Last Five Minutes, or the Countdown from Five.

The one factor I have not elaborated on at this time is the most important point of all. And that point is the *attitude* and *mind-set* of the prospect.

Is the prospect *ready? That* is what you must determine. And you determine it—

How else?

By being able to *read* the prospect's true attitude toward you and your product or service.

IS YOUR PROSPECT READY FOR THE CLOSE?

And so, with everything in place, you look across at your prospect, your future employer, your business associate. In the momentary lull in the conversation you find that he is seated in his swivel chair, legs crossed with his ankles linked, his arms on the arms of his chair, stroking his chin with one hand in a casual way. He's watching you. His eyes are clear, the pupils large. He's breathing normally, and he takes a moment to pat his hair into place by his ear. Now he removes his glasses a moment and looks over at you, tapping the frames on the edge of the desk.

QUESTION: What does this signify about the attitude and mind-set of the prospect?

ANSWER: It means he's *ready*. All the signs are positive. Go for it—hit him where it counts. And reel him in!

Perhaps I am being overoptimistic. Perhaps I sound too confident. Perhaps I tell you to go for a closing, and you succeed. But let me warn you, the chances are that your first closing will meet with some form of objection or stall. The odds are that you will not succeed.

In that case, answer the objection raised, and move on to your second closing. That's right—your *second* closing. To close you have to have at least a million possible closes in mind. If one doesn't work, you go on to another.

If the second closing brings up an objection, simply answer that objection the best you can, and move on to your third closing. By number five you probably will have your prospect. Here is a diagram of a typical series of exchanges in a sales interview at the point of closing:

SALESPERSON	PROSPECT
Greeting.	Greeting.
Question 1.	Answer.
Closing attempt 1.	Objection 1.
Answer. Closing attempt 2.	Objection 2.
Answer. Closing attempt 3.	Objection 3.
Answer. Question 2.	Answer.
Closing attempt 4.	Objection 4.
Answer. Closing attempt 5.	Agreement.

THE POSITIVE SIGNALS

The key to any person's positive attitude toward you is a relaxed and casual air. A casual attitude means that he or she is receptive toward your ideas and toward you as a person. People are different; some exhibit more casualness than others as a natural characteristic; others are more uptight as a general rule. But it is pretty evident that friendly and open behavior shows that a prospect is in an attitude of affirmation.

Let's look at the physical evidence of positive elements in the body language of the prospect:

- In general, he displays even, relaxed movements.
- He sits easily in his chair, and sometimes leans forward in an attitude of interest.
- He sits fairly still in a receptive attitude, swiveling about to face you as you move here and there in the room.
- His general facial expression is relaxed as he listens to you, with his mouth loose and not cramped tightly shut.
- Eye contact with you is relaxed and normal.
- The pupils of his eyes are wide and not narrowed. His gaze follows you about with interest, not suspicion.
- Occasionally he removes his glasses to look at you over them.
- He sits in his chair with his arms uncrossed, sometimes on the desk. His hands are open, not clenched tightly together.
- His expression is open; he does not put his hands or fists up in front of his face.
- His face and body are centered on you when you talk.
- He may bend over to tie a shoe, or brush lint off his trouser cuff.
- He sits easily, with his legs crossed casually, or his ankles crossed.
- He may stroke his chin as if to say, uh-huh.
- Generally, he is breathing normally and easily.
- If he is wearing a jacket and unbuttons it, or removes it, he is showing total confidence and trust in you. The same is true if he loosens his collar and tie.
- There is something on the desk obscuring his view

of you, and he reaches out and moves it aside.
(*Note:* this is a very good sign!)
- He leans promptly toward you to take a paper,
  pen, or sample you hand him.
- Suddenly he leans back in the chair and puts his
  feet up on the desk in a relaxed and genial mood.
- He gazes at the ceiling to recall something he is
  trying to remember to tell you.
- He becomes comradely and takes you over to an
  informal area of the office to show you a model of
  a yacht or something.
- He shows you a cup he won at golf.
- He pats his hair in place or scratches his ear.

. . . Or Maybe It Went This Way

Now, let's take another situation. Your prospect has been
prowling around the room during your presentation. In fact,
he's hardly looked at you during the whole spiel. You've seen
him tightening his tie, reaching down to button his jacket.
He has stood at the window looking out into the parking lot
for a few minutes during your interview. Now he sits down
in his chair, leaning forward, dead center of the desk, folding
his hands directly in front of him, staring at you.

> QUESTION: What does this group of signals mean?
> ANSWER: It means he's *against* you, against your
> product or your service—or you. Unless you can
> melt him down, you're dead meat.

These two examples are extreme, they are obviously too
simplistic to exist in real life, and they are freeze-frame
situations. That is, each takes place in a moment of time.
Generally speaking, you will have gone through all kinds of
different attitudes before the time you enter the prospect's
presence and the time you want to begin the closing.

You will probably have spotted half a dozen "no" signs,
and probably twice the number of "yes" signs. By mentally

adding them you can be sure that six to twelve means you should take a shot at it and go for it. It is best to take the shot, however, when you have the prospect in a relaxed and casual mood, rather than when he is completely uptight.

If for some reason, after a lot of positive signs, your prospect suddenly develops a stiff back and begins to beam you out of the office with a nasty look, try to bring him around somehow. Throw a joke into the hopper. Try to pull his mind away from whatever has seemed to bother him.

Then, when he is relaxed, go for it.

Every interview is a complete game in itself. The difference between one-on-one and a chess match is that you must read the prospect carefully as you go along; in a chess game, the pieces are in their proper squares on the board and you can see them and work out your true position clearly. In an interview—a person-to-person game—you must constantly assess and adjust to the attitude of your prospect. Any move toward a closing of the mind on the part of your prospect means that you must seek to open his or her mind once again to let you in.

THE NEGATIVE SIGNALS

The key to any person's negative attitude toward you is an uptight and belligerent air. A tense, hypercritical attitude means that he or she is unreceptive toward your ideas and toward you as a person. Some people may exhibit even more intense belligerence than others; some are simply uptight and vaguely annoyed. It is obviously pretty evident that being unfriendly and uptight shows that a prospect is in an attitude of negativity toward you and your product or service.

Let's look at some of these elements of negative body language more closely:

- In general, the prospect displays hostile, tensed-up movements. He may move awkwardly about, making sharp jerks with his body.

- He sits dead center of his desk, and clasps his hands in front of him, or crosses his arms over his chest. He reminds you of a court-martial judge about to pass the death sentence.
- Or he sits upright and hunched slightly forward with palms down on the desk, or hands folded tightly in front of him, putting up a defensive bulwark with his body.
- His general facial expression is grim, his mouth flat, his lips pulled in, his chin tucked in toward his throat, his jaws clenched.
- He normally avoids all eye contact, watching you warily out of the corner of the eye, and pretending not to see you at all.
- His eyes are narrowed, squinting at you. He even closes his eyes in long tight blinks as you talk to him.
- If he does not have his glasses on, he puts them on to keep you from seeing his eyes; he doesn't look at you anyway.
- He sits in his chair with his arms crossed, his body upright, his feet flat on the floor, his knees tightly together.
- He frequently uses his hands as masks for his face and hides his mouth and eyes as much as possible.
- He sometimes sits sideways to you, in a protective attitude, when you talk.
- He frowns constantly, his eyebrows knit tight. His eyelids are narrowed, the pupils pinpointed. His lips and mouth are tight, dry, and set hard.
- He sometimes supports his head with his hands. He may even put his hands behind his head, laced tight, making a pillow for his head.
- Generally, he breathes in deep, labored breaths, as if he had some obstruction in his throat. (He has; it's you!)
- He may even get up and put on his jacket, buttoning it tight in front of you, almost as if in confirmation of his obvious distrust of you.
- He may even reach over and bring something from

the edge of his desk to place it directly in front of him to screen you from view.

- He constantly puts his fingers to the side of his nose, expressing doubt. He rubs his nose a lot. He lifts his hand or index finger once in a while during your demonstration, and although he says nothing you know he disagrees with your points.
- He fails to lean forward and take anything you hand to him. Instead, he lets you drop it on the desk and then doesn't bother to take it up or look at it.
- He keeps getting up and walking around, looking out the window, and scratching and touching parts of his head or face.
- He drums with his fingers, rocks in his chair, hunches back, makes forward movements with his shoulders, moves about and turns away, and blinks a lot.
- He may smile when you haven't said anything funny. That means he is laughing at you, not with you. Or he may be a Cheshire Cat prospect: he starts in smiling at you and continues to do so from the beginning to the end. His smile is a mask. Unfortunately, unlike Alice's Cheshire Cat, he does not fade away. You do.
- He is boorish, and shakes his head occasionally to show you he disapproves, or yawns hugely, intentionally and unintentionally.
- He keeps clearing his throat and glancing around at other parts of the office. He keeps plucking lint off his clothes, scratches sudden itches, makes quick, jerky movements.
- He continues to swivel his chair away from you so that you see more of his side and back than you do of his face.

PENETRATING THE PROSPECT'S ROLE

You'll note that I have listed a lot more negative signals than I have positive ones. The reason should be obvious. When you're going well, you certainly know it. When you're not going well, you should be aware of it so you can do something about it *immediately*.

You'll recognize one important fact by now. Not only is the salesperson an actor of sorts, but so is the prospect. In other words, in an interview scene, both parties are playing roles. It is important for you to know the significant facets of the prospect's role and to recognize the signs that show you how you are doing from his point of view.

Some people are actors by instinct; others are not. If you are one of those who is not theatrical by nature, you must learn to read people and see through the masks they hold up to the world. If you feel you do not instinctively see through the people you deal with, then clip out the two preceding sections, positive and negative signals, and memorize them if you need to.

As you begin to apply these rules to your observations, you will pick up other signs I have not listed. That's natural. And as you continue to observe, you will realize that a little knowledge of what body signals mean can show you a great deal more about people than you ever knew before.

How to Bring Dissidents Around

You'll very soon learn to read assistance and negativism in a prospect. As soon as you detect it, you must try to break it down. How does a salesperson get through to a prospect who is totally negative?

I don't know where I read it, but I did see somewhere that Abraham Lincoln once said that if you want to win someone to your side of the argument, you must first of all convince him that you are his friend.

Easier said than done.

Dale Carnegie made a fortune out of telling people *How to Win Friends and Influence People* in a hugely successful best-seller many years ago. His idea for drawing people to you was to think more of them than of yourself. In other words, his main point was to phrase everything you said so that it tended to be a "you" sentence rather than an "I" sentence.

He had a lot more to say, but his key point was to extend your horizons outward to others; to give, by your presence, value to other people and their thoughts, ideas, and hopes. Take yourself out of things and put the other person into them.

A Little Christmas Music, Please

One of the best attitudes to assume when you see that your prospect is in a belligerent and negative mood is to exhibit friendship and affability toward him. Although a friendly opening with a real grump won't get you anywhere, it is likely that it may allow you to proceed. If you go in to an old grump as another old grump, you'll terminate the relationship immediately.

Bob Cratchit knew that. His Uncle Scrooge was one of the worst old grumps in Greater London. Cratchit treated him like a gentleman. After all, he was the boss. And in the end, the fact that Cratchit did not turn on the old bum and run a sharpened quill through his heart opened up a bright future for him eventually, once Scrooge's heart was thawed.

You start out being friendly, and anyone but an ossified jerk will respond at least in kind. You can never be sure. Your prospect, who is in a total negative state, may simply have had a bad morning. Breakfast toast burned to a crisp. Car wouldn't start. Elevator stalled at the eleventh floor for fifty minutes. Secretary spilled coffee on his desk. Client called up canceling a million-dollar order. My gosh, things happen!

Let a Smile Be Your Umbrella

People usually respond in a friendly manner eventually to a friendly overture. By being yourself a demonstration of a friendly person you more or less force the other person to respond similarly. If you continue unabashed to be civil and affable in the face of uncivil and boorish behavior, the prospect will become vaguely uncomfortable and will try to be nicer to you.

Work at it!

> YOU: Good morning, sir! (Wow! Who crossed you so badly this morning?)
>
> PROSPECT: What's good about it? (If you keep grinning like that, I'll smash your teeth in!)
>
> YOU: I always look forward to a day when I can do someone a bit of good. (I don't know about you, though!)
>
> PROSPECT: You can help me by closing the door quietly as you leave. (Right now!)
>
> YOU: Today you're my target of opportunity. (If you don't target me first!)
>
> PROSPECT: Well, I suppose I owe you a chance, anyway. (And then—go!)
>
> YOU: I appreciate that, sir. Now. . . .

On the other hand, if the prospect doesn't thaw, simply excuse yourself and make another date and withdraw. Certain days just aren't right for anything.

HOW TO COOL IT WHEN THINGS ARE HOT

There's another situation that can develop in the general give-and-take of an interview. Luckily it doesn't happen much. But when it does—watch out!

I'm referring to a situation in which the prospect suddenly becomes angry at you. You, in turn, aren't really aware of how angry the prospect is, or you are inattentive and allow the exchange to accelerate into a real shouting match before you can stop it.

When this happens, you *must* defuse it.

Seven Steps to a Cooling-Off

I have dreamed up a number of rules for dealing with such an incendiary situation. I hope you never get yourself into such a mess, but it does happen. If it comes up, pay attention to these points:

1. Be aware, as early as you can, of the anger that is building up in your prospect. This reflects back on what this whole chapter is about: reading other people. You should be able to see the rage beginning to consume your prospect before it breaks out into the open. Remember that there are two ways to fight anger: by running away, and by fighting back. Make sure you realize that the anger is building and is about to break loose.

2. Study your own reactions. For example, if you are becoming heated too, if your heartbeat is accelerating—say above 100—watch out! Make sure you are able to keep yourself from losing your temper before you react to your prospect's break. And make sure you are aware of what is going to happen before it does happen.

3. When the break comes, hold your immediate response. Do not say *anything*. Let the prospect's rage surface and blow. Listen carefully to what the prospect is saying. Try to analyze the reason for his anger. Try to see where he is trying to go with it. Remember that he is fighting back somehow—but, against what? Find out what he is fighting back *at*.

4. Ask for time to stop and think. In other words, call a momentary truce. If you respond in any other way—say, if you too blow up and begin to fight your prospect word for word, gesture for gesture, point for point—you will get absolutely nowhere. Both of you will simply exhaust your-selves and the interview will self-destruct. Do not allow this to happen!

5. As you cool your prospect, think to yourself: "What do I want to happen?" Ask yourself how you can turn his confrontation into a rational discussion of the problem that has surfaced. Think as calmly as you can about how you can bring reason to this emotional cock-up.

6. If your prospect is riding the crest of a wave of rage, do not do anything until he finally runs out of breath or stops to gain thinking time. Never fuel the rage of another individual by fighting back. Make yourself as neutral as possible. Quite soon the prospect will realize he is doing all the yelling and all the acting. His own sense of proportion will assert itself and he will at least calm down. You may not get an apology, but you'll quite soon earn peace and quiet.

7. Realize that explanations will not really help. You must find a way to get your prospect to tell what has angered him and then allow yourself time to find some way to discuss the situation rationally. In good time you can come up with some answer. You know that; you have to convince *him* of the fact.

Controlling the Rest of the Interview

Now go into these positive steps to get the conversation back on the track:

1. Once you learn what your prospect is angry about, ask him what he wants you to do about it. Listen to him when he is talking to you. Let him know that you're listening carefully. When the two of you are both on a normal plane, then go to the next step.

2. Restate the problem. Discuss the problem together, with all the ramifications you can determine. Then restate the problem once again, so that it is clear to your prospect as to what exactly you think is involved.

3. Examine your prospect's needs and desires, and listen again to what he wants from you. Make sure he knows you are listening to him. Force him to speak slowly and clearly.

4. Tell him what you want from him in return for what you are going to do for him. You are now on a rational level, and are discussing the situation the way two people should discuss a situation.

5. Negotiate. You can go on from here the way you would have been going before anger interrupted the interview.

6. In some way, devise a means to save your prospect's face. Otherwise he will feel that he has made himself look the fool by exploding and losing his temper. Make him feel better about his loss of control.

7. Get a verbal acknowledgment of what you have both agreed to in you negotiations. Make sure that the two of you are absolutely agreed now. Put it down in writing. Do not make your prospect sign the agreement, but make sure that he sees exactly what you have set down in writing.

8. Now that everything is settled, make sure that you let your prospect have the last word. Do not let him dismiss you without making him feel that he is the winner in this exchange. By the same token, do not make him feel that he has won by throwing a childish tantrum. It is best not to let him think of the explosion at all.

RECOGNIZING THE TURNING POINT

For a brief recapitulation of how to establish the proper turning point in the interview, let's begin with what you have accomplished up to this point:

- You have successfully established a feeling of rapport with your prospect.
- You have listened to your prospect and led him through the steps of your presentation.
- You have studied your prospect as closely as possible all during your interview.

- You have probed your prospect to determine that he feels affirmative as you have surmised.
- You have asked specific questions in response to certain body language attitudes to determine how close your emotional appeals are to the mark.
- You have finished your presentation and determined that the prospect has all the necessary data.

Now comes the crucial point of the interview. Everything points toward the proper time for starting a closing move.

But *is* it really the time?

It's a simple enough thing to find out.

How do you do it?

Put Your Prospect under a Microscope

You may be lucky. Your prospect may utter these fabulous words:

"You've sold me. I'm convinced. Let's get down to the nitty-gritty. There's no use going into any more selling high jinks. I've got my pen. Just give me the papers to sign."

That doesn't usually happen. Most prospects *hate* to spend money. Most prospects keep their real feelings bottled up inside them, because they know that it isn't good to appear too eager.

But you have ways of determining these bottled-up feelings, haven't you? Sure! You can *read* the prospect. And now, if the signs look right, it's closing time!

Pay particular attention to *these* messages:

- The prospect looks wistfully at the product and then looks back at it, out of the corners of his eyes. (He's playing a game with himself, and he's losing it.)
- He licks his lips; they're dry from the struggle not to buy.

- He inhales deeply, readying himself to take the plunge.
- His face lights up. His expression brightens. His eyes are soft and large.
- He seems to be preening himself, congratulating himself on his good taste.
- He goes over and touches the product, looking at it long and hard.
- He suddenly breaks down and grins like the cat that just got into the cream jar.

If you see any of those signs in the prospect—or any two of them together—you can be sure he's sold. You've got him. You can begin spending your commission.

But be sure to close with him first!

How?

By reading the next chapter.

The Sales Interview: Countdown from Five

You're all set to go.

You've recognized the turning point. You know your prospect is ready. There is nothing more to do but move on ahead.

And yet . . . and yet . . .

At this point it's always best to let your mind rove back over all your preparations to make sure you haven't forgotten some key factor that would tend to ruin the sale.

The following are the questions you ask yourself.

Did You Represent Your Product Faithfully?

Have you gone over the features of your product or service completely with your prospect? Have you noted its features, pointed out its advantages, neutralized its disadvantages, cited its benefits?

Have you been completely honest with your prospect? Have you admitted the shortcomings of the product or service as well as stressed the superior elements? Have you put together an honest profile of it?

Have you balanced the product against its competition in a careful and straightforward fashion? Have you placed your product or service in its proper competitive position within the industry?

Have you been diligent in discussing its value in relation to the competition and to other products or services in the same field?

If you have, then you have successfully carried out your duties in knowing your product or service and in representing it honestly to your prospect.

Did You Qualify Your Prospect Correctly?

Have you honestly studied your prospect in a way that will have determined objectively how much he or she needs your product or service? Have you honestly weighed the benefits such a product or service will provide the prospect?

Have you determined the proper price the prospect is willing to and can pay for your product? Have you compared the prospect's ability to pay with the cost of the model you have settled on?

Have you found out what the prospect already owns and discovered what features of your product will help him or her out? Have you discovered which benefits of your product most appeal to the prospect? Have you discovered which features of your product *least* appeal to the prospect?

Have you made the proper search of the prospect's background to find out what improvement is needed in the product or service now owned or used? Will your product or service help improve his or her operation?

Have you made sure that there are no hidden obstacles that might crop up during your final discussions with the prospect? No specters that might rise like ghosts of Christmas Past to destroy the sale?

If so, then you have successfully carried out your duties in regard to knowing and qualifying your prospect so that you can honestly represent your product or service to him or her.

Did You Control the Conversation Successfully?

Have you mastered the various forms of the interrogatory in order to keep a firm control of the conversation? Have you varied the constructions so as not to make the trick of asking questions obvious?

Have you used the technique of interrogation to its fullest in eliciting information from your prospect? Have you used questions to help establish a bond between yourself and the prospect?

Have you determined from your questions exactly what the prospect *needs* in the product and service? Have you made the decision for him or her as to what model of the product or service is needed?

If so, you have carried out your questioning technique successfully and can move on to the next area of the interview.

Did You Cope Successfully with the Prospect's Objections?

Have you properly disregarded and ignored simple stall tactics masquerading as objections? Have you successfully identified objections that are real and answered them as cogently as you possibly could?

Have you dealt with the handful of very real objections that surfaced during your sales exchange? Have you heard out, picked apart, and finally answered the objections that really counted?

Have you managed to deal honestly with the all-important subject of the price of the product or service? Have you pointed out how cheapness in a product or service does not actually save you money in the long run?

If so, you have managed your way through the minefield of objections that have surfaced and are ready to bring your interview to a close.

Did You Get to the Heart of the Prospect?

Have you been able to arouse one or more emotional responses in your prospect in order to make him or her *want* the product or service you represent? Have you actually used psychological means to make your prospect change from a skeptic to a believer?

Have you been able to utilize your understanding of psychological motivations enough to be able to persuade your prospect, without badgering or forcing him or her, to honestly desire your product or service?

Have you truly aroused a hard psychological interest in your product or service so that the prospect is wholeheartedly willing to purchase it from you?

If so, you have mastered the art of getting to the heart of the prospect.

Did You Recognize the Turning Point?

Have you been able to pierce the mask that your prospect holds up to the world in order to read accurately how he or she feels about your product or service? Have you read the prospect's body language with enough in-depth perception to see when he or she is ready to close?

Have you interpreted the positive and negative body

signals in enough detail to bring forth objections and hesitations that can help you deal with whatever is bothering the prospect?

Have you been able to bring a dissenting prospect around to your way of thinking, once you were able to analyze his or her true feelings about you and your product?

Have you been able to cool down a prospect who has suddenly lost his or her temper in front of you during a discussion of some unimportant detail? Have you defused this incipient time bomb and brought the conversation back to normal communication levels?

Have you been able to recognize the turning point? Have you been able to guarantee the fact that your prospect is at the crucial point and needs only to be led straight into the closing phase of the sale?

If so, you are ready for the final closing moves. You are ready to undertake the end game. You are ready to start the countdown from five.

THE PURPOSE OF CLOSING

Let's for the moment consider the unmentionable. The "unmentionable" is usually the sum of money that the prospect *really* doesn't want to spend. The unmentionable is usually the price *and* the contractual documents that make the sale weasel-proof. The unmentionable usually comes in the form of a nasty little package of papers; in plain words, it is a bill of sale, a contract, a binding agreement.

Villains in Victorian dramas used to ruin widows by stealing documents labeled "DEEDS" through which they would force the widows to surrender their beautiful daughters to unwanted marriages with evil old men.

I must be frank about it. Money is the thing we are all here on earth to earn, at least in our capitalist slice of the globe. Money is the reason for all this talk and activity. Money buys the things we want. Money feeds us, clothes us, keeps us alive.

It is not chic to *mention* it. Nobody wants to admit it is a necessity. Because a contract of sale involves the eventual handing over of money, nobody wants to *see* it, no matter how beautiful it appears and how neatly it is typed up.

The Obscenity of the Closing Scene

Closing means getting the prospect to sign a contract, or to hand over money in a bundle. This concentration on money is *obscene*. People palpitate and shake and have cardiac arrests thinking about money.

For that reason, because you are dealing with one of life's most obnoxious articles—dirty old money, or an agreement to part with filthy lucre—you must not let this awful thing appear suddenly or unexpectedly in front of the pristine eyes of your prospect.

Keep the dreaded paper locked tightly in the drawer until the *right* moment.

I guarantee it: If you want to *lose* a sale you've worked hard to set up for hours, days, or weeks, you have only to do one thing. Open your desk drawer, pull out the papers of agreement, and slap them down on the desk in front of your prospect.

"Sign there!"

The Secret of the Locked Drawer

The prospect will turn pale. Perspiration will pop out on his skin. His eyes may roll up into his skull. He may fall back in horror. He may collapse to the carpet. He may even reel toward the door to make a final and inexorable exit from your life.

I won't go into his possible comments.

On pain of death—do not flash a previously unseen contract on an unwary prospect.

Keep reminding yourself that, although you have worked from the first moment of your acquaintance with this prospect, be it male or female, and that you have made every possible overture to smooth the way for a final settlement of a sale, you must never flash a contract in front of his or her eyes without the proper introductory phrases.

The contract is safely ensconced—out of sight!—in a drawer, in a file, or under a pile of innocent-looking papers. Now you must bridge the distance between yourself and your knowledge that the prospect is ready *and* the final revelation—voilà!—of the dark and evil contract that the prospect must sign with his or her blood.

The Playing of the All-Important End Game

To bridge the distance you must propose the proper steps in the form of what is universally known as "a closing" or "closings."

You will note that at this point the end game has commenced. It is different from chess pieces on a board. It is rather like some kind of intricate dance step, a mating ritual of dragons and dames, a gavotte of sugarplum fairies.

But it must be danced. And you, as the leader of the dance, must know exactly how to charm, romance, and *propose* to the prospect for an effective marriage.

WHAT IS A CLOSING?

To simplify the matter and drain all the mystique out of it: a closing is simply a document of commitment between seller and buyer.

It is the final capitulation in the courtship game that has been played between seller and buyer during the long and protracted hours of verbal intercourse.

Essentially, the seller is down on the knees with the buyer, with the old-fashioned phrase trembling on his lips: "Will you marry me?"

Instead of marriage, he is proposing purchase. "Will you buy my product?"

> *Note:* I see I have committed a grave faux pas already by comparing a closing to a proposal of marriage. In no way am I suggesting that the seller is automatically male, the buyer always female. Exactly the opposite can be true. Or both seller and buyer may be male; or both may be female. Nevertheless, the parallel *is* apt. Please forgive me and read on.

The Closing: Its Verbal Aspects

Although the typical closing involves a number of basic elements, the most important aspect for the salesperson is the verbal. The question immediately arises: How do you tell the prospect that it is time to make a commitment? How do you prepare the prospect for the bloodletting that is the writing of the signature on the paper?

Over the years various salespersons have experimented with a number of different "closings," that is, verbal techniques that lead the prospect into the final signatory.

I like to look at these verbal forays as the final moves in a chess game, the famous end game. I also like to think of these closing moves as essential elements in the last five minutes of any sales campaign.

And so the three combine to introduce the final and most crucial phase of the sales interview:

- The verbal closing
- The end game
- The contractual commitment

The Balance Sheet Close

Tom Hopkins, one of today's most successful salespersons, and a master at teaching others how to become sales champions, calls the "Balance Sheet Close" one of the oldest in the business.

You can study it for some idea of how to develop your own; or you can utilize it as it stands.

It's sometimes used when all else fails, when, for some reason, your prospect has suddenly balked after an almost surefire capitulation to your presentation. Suddenly doubt creeps into him or into her. You realize instinctively that unless you come up with a winning closure, you've just lost your prospect.

Balancing the Yeses and the Noes

The idea of the balance sheet is one of the simplest of all decision-makers. The crux of the closing is to show the prospect that all signs favor purchase of the product or service, not rejection.

Because it involves pencil and paper—and words—you can make it work more easily because the props help take the prospect's mind off his own indecision: which is what is holding up everything, anyway. He or she *wants* to be persuaded—right? *You* know it's a yes. Only the prospect doesn't.

1. Draw a vertical line down the center of a sheet of typing paper. On the left-hand side, write the word: FAVOR-ABLE. On the right-hand side, write the word: UNFAVORA-BLE.

2. As you draw up your diagram of the "balance sheet," you talk to the prospect.

> "Sometimes it's hard to make up your mind. My uncle used to show me a trick he learned years ago. He'd write down all the reasons *for* an action; and all the reasons *against* an action. Then he'd put them down on opposite sides of a sheet of paper."

And you show the prospect the balance sheet you've drawn.

3. You tell the prospect you're going to put down all the reasons to buy your product or service in the left-hand column. As you put each reason down—after all, you've got them right there in your head, since you were the one who brought them up!—you discuss it fully to find if there are any flaws in your argument.

The prospect nods and agrees with you as you do so.

4. Now comes the crucial move. You hand your pencil or pen to the prospect. You instruct the prospect to write down all the reasons *not* to buy the product. You can see the strategy here. By letting the prospect handle the dissenting points, you've brought him or her into the discussion, and made this action a critical part of the "balance sheet."

As you watch, the prospect puts down all the arguments *against* purchase of the product. You urge the prospect on, should he or she falter. You're in full cooperation, of course, even though these actions are pushing your possible sale out into limbo.

Now the prospect has finished the list of reasons not to buy.

5. You put the sheet down in front of the prospect and both of you study it. Then, point by point, you go over the pluses and the minuses. In each case, you discuss with your prospect the details of the yeses and the noes.

You're finished.

"Well, let's see now. We've pretty well gone over everything here. I can count the reasons to buy—there are ten of them. On the other hand, I see only four against. Can you think of any more?"

If you've done this right, the prospect cannot think of any more at all. You may have thought of a few, but at this point it's not nice to bring these out into plain sight.

6. This is an important step. Do not muff it. It requires a great deal of self-control. Pay strict attention to what I tell you here, and do not deviate from it. *To deviate is to forfeit the game.*

You stare at the columns of comments and you tap the paper where you have written down the totals with the point of the pen: 10 to 4.

And you say: "Don't you think the answer here is pretty obvious?"

Now comes the crucial part. You state the question, and from that moment on *you remain silent!*

I mean—absolutely silent! If you open your mouth before your prospect, you lose the match!

7. The prospect sheepishly nods and admits that indeed the odds are that he or she should probably purchase the product.

It's the beginning of the end. You have closed. And now you bring out the order pad or the contract and let the prospect see it and figure out what it is.

After the proper amount of handling it and letting the prospect think about it and get used to it, you lay it down on the desk, find a pen somewhere, and hand it over.

It's all done. You've made your closing.

Countdown from Five is over.

Refinements on the Balance Sheet Closing

You'll find that a lot of old-timers in the business feel this closing is one of the most ancient and timeworn of all closings. But don't let that discourage you. If you happen to utilize it, and find someone laughing at you, laugh right along with him or her.

And win!

Talk about it. Yes, it's old—but it's fairly effective.

And so on.

Actually, it's been called a lot of things other than the "Balance Sheet" Closing. It's known popularly as the "Benjamin Franklin Close," with some salespersons attributing it to Ben Franklin himself. The use of the name Ben Franklin gives the closing some personality.

"Now Ben Franklin was one of our most astute thinkers. But occasionally even he couldn't quite make up his mind about certain things. And in order to find out if he really wanted to do something when he was hesitant about it, he'd put down the yeses in one column and the noes in another." And so on.

Treat this one any way you want. It's old, but it's solid. Don't let anybody laugh you out of it once you've started. Laugh *with* the prospect—and let the format win him over.

HEDGING THE BETS JUST A BIT

Actually, I have probably been a bit too optimistic, talking about a closing as quick and easy as the Balance Sheet Close. Chances are, really, that your first attempt at a close will fail.

The prospect will immediately come up with another objection of some kind that will stall your end game.

Remember: there is more than one closing.

If Closing Number 1 fails, move on to Closing Number 2—or wherever your imagination leads you.

The main point I'm making is this:

Never dream you are going to end the game and checkmate your prospect with only one move. You may need five. You may need even more than that.

Always have a number of them in your mind, ready to pull out and put to use in case another objection arises. Then, when one fails, you reorganize your thoughts a bit, and move on to the next one.

Redeploying Your Troops

When your first closing attempt has failed, there are at least three things you must do immediately.

- Smooth over the failure.
- Go over the good points.
- Ask a transition question.

Smoothing Over the Failure. You recognize the fact that your closing move has failed. In fact, your prospect too may have realized that it was a closing move and that it did not get anywhere. Your purpose now is not to *admit* failure; your purpose is to move full-steam ahead.

> "Perhaps I have been moving a little too fast in these crucial stages. I should apologize for my zeal. I know my product is good and I know how much it will help you. Yet I don't want to *push* you—even if it is for your own good."

And so forth. Once you have apologized for moving too fast, you have really smoothed over your own failure—without admitting it was a failure.

Now you can go ahead to the second item.

Going Over the Good Points. You have been moving ahead directly to a commitment. Now you must back off just a bit. The best way to back off and to forfeit none of the ground gained is to recapitulate all the good points both you and the prospect are agreed upon.

At this juncture, you summarize the benefits that will accrue to the prospect if the product or service is purchased. This is a neutralizing move, performed to stall for time and to bring the prospect into line for another closing attempt.

Point by point, you take the prospect over *all* the agreed-upon advantages of the product. You discuss each one, using the proper confirmatory at the end of each statement:

> "Now we are agreed on the particular model you wanted, aren't we? And aren't we of a mind about the size you wanted?"

And so on.

At the end of this inventory of the good points, you have succeeded in reminding the prospect of all the pluses. Play it cool and let the discussion move on its own. It will. Once the list is complete, you're ready to move on to the transitional question that moves you into your second attempt at closing.

Asking the Transitional Question. The transitional question can be couched in almost any kind of language. It is simply a restatement of all the things you have been discussing during the summary of the benefits and advantages of the product.

In fact, the question is almost a kind of bridge to the second closing attempt.

> "I feel we've more or less considered most of the points so that we're in sync with one another. I feel we've finally come to an agreement of the minds on them, haven't we?"

And then you start your second closing.

Which one?

Well, there are dozens of them. They're not all as complex as the Balance Sheet Closing—some, in fact, require only a short sentence or two.

Let's look at a number of these and study what makes them work.

THE ORDER PAD CLOSE

This is one of the simplest closes there is. All you need are the right kinds of props. And all you have to do is *lead* the prospect to ask certain questions about the product. But with the proper utilization of the interrogative technique discussed in Chapter 5, you'll be able to accomplish that.

First, there are two props necessary:

- An order-form pad
- A ballpoint pen

Second, you have to lead the prospect to pose a question about the product—any question, really.

> YOU: My teenage daughter can't spell worth a darn.
> I guess that's why she *loves* this program.
> PROSPECT: Oh! That reminds me. Does the software include a spell-check?

Or:

> YOU: (flicking a handkerchief carefully over the top of the floor computer monitor, with a rueful smile) These computers tend to be great dust collectors.

PROSPECT: By the way. Does the monitor come with a dust cover?

Once you have elicited a question from the prospect— again, *any* question—it's a simple matter to proceed.

You smoothly exhibit an order form from wherever it has remained in hiding and begin to scribble in words.

PROSPECT: Does the software include a spell-check?
YOU: Would you *prefer* software with a spell-check?
PROSPECT: Yes.
YOU: I'd like to make a note of that.
PROSPECT: Hey! I never said I'd buy it! What are you doing with that pen and pad?
YOU: I simply cannot remember details. I have to write everything down. I wouldn't want to give you something you don't want, would I?

It may seem a bit crass, but you'll find that most of the time it works. You usually don't need another closing.

THE ROGUE'S GALLERY CLOSE

I like to file my toughest case histories on a bulletin board I've rigged up in a back room. On little three-by-five file cards I write up a short summary of each difficult case and pin it up for some time.

If I am engaged in a sales campaign of a similar nature, I frequently run back over my so-called Rogue's Gallery of cases to see what kind of approach finally closed the sale.

Quite frequently, I'll pull out of my memory bank a complex exchange, and maybe even reminisce with the prospect about it. Usually, though, I can get enough from the basic story to turn the prospect in the right direction.

If a product has made a particularly notable improvement in any prospect's business, I can always tell the story with the actual facts and figures at my command. *That* kind of recommendation *counts*.

THE REVERSE ENGLISH CLOSE

We already went over the petty excuses people come up with for not wanting to spend their money: Objections of the First Kind. I've discovered that the same ploy works in reverse in a closing. Understand that this gambit is really not a priority type of closing to use; it's the kind of thing you fall back on if all else fails—a kind of last-bullet maneuver before the end.

It goes this way:

PROSPECT: I'm going to sleep on this.

Instinctively, you think: This one's going to get away. Stop! Don't go! On the other hand—why force the prospect's hand. Why not . . . ?

YOU: I couldn't agree more. You want to take some extra time to think about this—it's obviously that important to you.
PROSPECT: Well, I guess it is. Yeah. You're right.

The prospect is on the hook. You don't let up.

YOU: Now you're going to give this a lot of the heaviest kind of consideration, aren't you?
PROSPECT: Uh. Well—yes.

Pull up a little on the hook. Set the teeth on edge. Play it put-upon. Pull a long face. You lost!

YOU: You're not trying to bow out of this transaction, are you?
PROSPECT: Oh, no! Everything's fine!

Now jerk hard on the line. Let it all hang out. Your prospect has hurt your feelings. He's done you in!

> YOU: Just so we both know where we're coming from, exactly what is it you want to think over? Is it the company? Is it the product? Is it *me?*
>
> PROSPECT: Of course not! Don't worry—

Dig in more deeply. Ask specific questions about the product, the service. New objections may surface—and if they do, handle them. Suggested Rereading: Chapter 5.

THE OPEN CLOSE

This close is reminiscent of the Reverse English Close, although it's entirely different. It *could* be considered a cutesy-pie close, except that it really isn't.

The psychology is clear-cut and incisive. You're working toward your close. You suddenly stop, and smile vaguely. You mention that you just remembered a situation that occurred last month.

You had a prospect that was completely qualified for the service you're selling. But right in the middle of the negotiations, you were suddenly apprised by the bank that there would be trouble financing the purchase.

You drop that line of thought, and switch back to your presentation. You lead the prospect up to the close, and just before you begin a conventional close, you look at the prospect, chuckle nervously, and say:

> YOU: You're quite sure you *are* able to swing the amount of money this service will cost, aren't you? I don't want you to be trying too hard. I know you want it, but—Well, don't get your hopes *too* high.

And the prospect immediately assures you he *can* pay for it. So you close:

> YOU: Let's stop all this talk and act. You fill out the application and we can tell if there's going to be any trouble. How about that?

Of course: Sure.

THE BIG NAME CLOSE

In your Rogue's Gallery you have one or two sales of which you're inordinately proud: they are Big Fish that you hooked. They are people at the top of their professions. They are Big Names.

You revisit one of your Big Names to discuss further possibilities, and to make sure everything is going well with the product or service you originally sold him.

In the course of the conversation, you ask the Big Name if he's willing to share his knowledge of the machines you represent with other people in the industry. Most probably he will assure you he will. And he says he doesn't mind getting a call from someone about your product.

Soon you visit the prospect you want to sell, and you mention the Big Name and how much *he* likes your product. You work the conversation around and soon the prospect is on the telephone to the Big Name, talking about the sale.

And so you close.

THE DOUBLE-EDGED CLOSE

You remember the close I blew in the first chapter? Actually, I developed that close *because* I had blown a fairly easy closing effort.

I call it the Double-Edged Close now, and use it fairly frequently.

It's a close that you back into. Nevertheless, by controlling the conversation with the use of questions, questions, questions, you can almost cause the prospect to ask the question the way mine did those long years ago:

PROSPECT: Can you deliver after ten days' notice?

And, of course, by now you know the proper answer to that. It's another question!

YOU: Shall I have it sent to the main office or to the branch we were talking about?

Don't forget, it's very easy to answer a question with a simple affirmative statement. Never do that in a sales interview! Always try to twist the answer into another question. Always!

THE UNMENTIONABLE

You'll remember I pointed out in the middle of this chapter that you should never let the order book, the contract, or the papers of commitment *appear* before their proper curtain cue.

The best time to bring these unattractive props out is during the beginning of your closing spiel. Let the prospect see them as you drag them out, but do not mention them by name. Your verbal flow will carry the prospect along so that the sudden appearance of the contract or order form will seem natural and not frightening.

The idea is not to terrify the prospect by the unexpected flash of a bulky and formidable contract. Even the sight of an order form can cause chills and cold sweat.

Work the appearance of this unmentionable into your dialogue. I would suggest that you practice adroitly removing an order form from a drawer or cabinet *as you speak* in order to get the proper synchronization of speech and action down pat.

It must not seem to be a practiced move. It should be smooth and natural.

THE SALES INTERVIEW: THE LAST FIVE MINUTES

There you have it. I've given you a number of closings to choose from to make your own in any way you wish. You'll probably come up with a number of your own once you get used to controlling those final five minutes that are so crucial to any sale.

Remember that the closing move can never stand alone. It must be accompanied by all the earlier research, study, and practice you have put into the elements discussed in this book.

By the same token, there can be no slacking up in the closing moves. They must be as crisp and clear as the earlier actions taken to *prepare* for the closing.

Neither can stand alone. Each must be accompanied by the other for success.

And you must find your success here in the last five minutes; it cannot come any sooner—nor any later.

9

The Job Interview: Countdown from Five

The job interview is similar in almost all its aspects to the sales interview. The manifest difference, of course, is the fact that in the sales interview it is the product or the service that is up for purchase. In the job interview, it is the individual himself or herself who is up for purchase.

- In the sales interview you sell a product or a service.
- In the job interview you sell *yourself*.

Because the two interviews are similar except for minor details, it follows that you can use the same techniques and ploys used to sell a product in order to sell yourself. In fact, there is a remarkable similarity between the job interview and the chess game—the opening gambit, the middle game, and the end game.

For the moment, let's run through these similarities before coming to the crucial encounter: the last five minutes of the job interview.

KNOW YOUR PRODUCT = KNOW YOURSELF

If you had lived in ancient times and had been about to seek a new job, you would have sought help not from an employment counselor, but from the gods. The gods were in charge of running the world. They managed personal problems as well as business problems. They were all-powerful. You approached them through temples called "oracles," at which human beings acting as mediums between heaven and earth interpreted the will of the gods to individuals seeking help or guidance.

The most famous oracle was located at Delphi, in Phocis, Greece, right on the lower slopes of Mount Parnassus, which the ancient gods called home. Although it might have been assumed to be graffiti, there was a saying on the wall of the oracle at Delphi that has been handed down through the ages. Plutarch, that most famous Roman biographer, historian, and writer, said that "all other precepts" of life depended on that one phrase.

The phrase was:

Know thyself.

Menander, a Greek playwright, added his own bit of wisdom to the original aphorism:

In many ways the saying "Know thyself" is not well said. It is more practical to say: "Know other people."

Truth to tell, by knowing yourself, you *do* know others. No man is an island. We are all part of the continent. We are all extensions of each other.

By truly knowing yourself, you are able to estimate your strengths and your weaknesses. By these estimates, you are able to understand what features of your personality to put forward, what to hold in reserve.

Knowing yourself means "getting it all together" for viewing by others—in particular, by your prospective employer. Not only must you get it all together, but you must get it all together with each part in sync with the other.

Synchronize Your Outer and Inner Selves

- Body language must parallel verbal language.
- Personal hygiene and grooming must project personal integrity.
- Dress must establish a sense of what is appropriate and right for the business scene.
- Attitude must project politeness, courtesy, and friendliness.
- Be rested and be punctual: get a good night's sleep and eat a good breakfast before setting out.

These are basic facts known by everyone, but it is surprising how many times people forget to check themselves out thoroughly before putting their best foot forward.

> *Moral:* What good's a best foot forward when the rest of the persona is flawed and backward?

KNOW YOUR PROSPECT = KNOW YOUR POTENTIAL EMPLOYER

As the salesperson qualifies the prospect to whom he is selling a product or service, so the job seeker researches and investigates the potential employer he is going to be interviewed by for a job.

Not only should the job seeker find out all he can about

the person conducting the interview, but he or she should find out as much as possible about the company for whom the interviewer works.

In seeking information about the company and the position for which you are vying, you can research information in several specific areas:

- Annual report
- Business plan
- Job description
- Job objectives

You can spend some time in the library checking out the company, too:

- Dun and Bradstreet's *Million Dollar Directory*
- *Value Line*
- Standard and Poor's corporation records
- Trade publications
- Industry directories
- Industry journals

Check through your own personal working network. It is quite likely that someone you know has primary or secondary sources of information; perhaps he or she can forward data to you about the individual you are going to be interviewed by. Learn all you can about whatever quirks the individual exhibits. Learn his or her likes and dislikes. Learn all you can to give your own presentation of yourself the proper direction and exposure.

Qualifying the interviewer parallels qualifying the prospect in most of its phases. Being forewarned is being forearmed against possible slipups or interview gaffes.

COPING WITH OBJECTIONS = COPING WITH EMERGENCIES

No matter how carefully you orchestrate your presentation of "you" in the best possible light, things can go wrong.

While a buyer may bring up objections to the seller, an interviewer may find unexpected flaws in the real you.

How do you cope with the unexpected?

For the moment let's explore the point a little more fully in a story having to do with a job interview. This one concerns the semiretired Axel Redivivus and his attempt to get a sales manager job with a top firm.

AXEL REDIVIVUS

Axel had been one of the top sales personalities of his day, but he had moved up in the corporate structure and was not required to go on the road anymore. However, a conglomerate bought up the company for which he worked, and when push came to shove, Axel was on the bricks.

He could have retired, but he wanted to get back into selling. He missed the give and take of the game; he missed not meeting new people. He decided to make a try to get back in. His age was against him, but he figured he could overcome that by a good aggressive style.

I really went out on the limb for him. When he came to me for help to get an interview with our top brass—we needed a new sales director—I agreed to put my reputation on the line for him. I hoped, along with Axel, that he would succeed and not make an ass of himself.

The problem was, our guys were all young and aggressive—yuppies with excellent sales records. Youth was their thing. Axel knew that. His point of view was that age and experience were as necessary as youth and energy, that age could afford a kind of symbolic balance between the generations. But—old gray beards? Golden oldies?

Murder, He Wrote

In the event, Axel came on strong. The brass was seated around a huge boardroom table, all eyeing him as he came in. I watched with some apprehension, but they were looking at Axel, hardeyed, slit-pupiled, almost like dogs sniffing the new mongrel on the block.

Our CEO finally called on Axel after making some preliminary remarks about the presentation he was going to make, and Axel approached the table confidently. He glanced up and down the row of those young, wide-open, freshly scrubbed faces, and took a deep breath. I was dying inside for him—dying!

The Point Is, Ladies and Gentlemen—

Reaching into his pocket, he removed a ballpoint pen, and held it in his hand as if to make a gesture with it. Well, he dropped it, just as he was about to go to work with it. It tinkled on the hard floor. I don't know what Axel had in mind, but I realized he had to retrieve that pencil gracefully to go on. He leaned down—and I knew how his bones creaked and his back ached—got the pencil, and came up with it.

Disaster struck.

As he rose slowly from that awkward position, his head hit the bottom of the oak table edge *hard*, caught his head-piece—I didn't even *know* he was bald!—and flipped it over so it hung down in front of his eyes like a forelock. He stood there, stunned, and the headpiece slowly loosened from his bald pate and floated down onto the boardroom table surface, where it lay quivering.

My heart absolutely seized up. I was dying—for myself as well as for Axel. No one would ever forget this moment. I was afraid to look around at the merriment in the eyes of those young clods as they stared at the Grand Old Man who wasn't really so grand anymore but was a Bald Old Fudd. I looked around; they were stifling their laughter. I wanted to kill them—and myself.

What could a man do? As for me—

"So much for dramatic beginnings," Axel said with a cool smile. "The product I'm going to tell you about doesn't *need* gimmicks to sell it." He reached out his hand. "Young sir, if you'll hand me my Jack Benny, I'll be glad to continue."

A rather stunned Yuppie handed him his hair, which he thrust negligently in his pocket. Axel pointed with his ballpoint pen. "Now, let's get on with the product."

And he did—without missing a beat!

Talk about snatching victory from the jaws of defeat!

The Problem of Control

Axel did get the job with us. His ability to rebound from calamity convinced even the callowest of those salespersons that he was worth his salt no matter what his chronological age. *Or* his image.

That's enough about catastrophes and emergencies. Generally speaking, you won't have any as disastrous as those two. But they do crop out; when they do, you must try to control them as completely and nonchalantly as you can. Be cool. It helps cover over the most embarrassing of emergencies.

Let's move on to an area where your control over yourself—as nearly always—is of primary importance, and does not depend on a quick, intuitive, ingenious recovery from a cataclysm of unmitigated proportions.

CONVERSATION CONTROL = SELF-CONTROL

Your technique in maintaining control of the conversation involves maintaining control of yourself more than maintaining control over the interviewer. There is no apt parallel here between the sales interview and the job interview.

- In a sales conversation, *you* deliberately lead the buyer.
- In a job interview, you allow yourself to be *led* by the interviewer.

You are the interrogatee; your interviewer is the interrogator. You come prepared to reveal what your interviewer wants to know or to see.

Here are some tips on maintaining control over yourself:

BODY LANGUAGE. Make sure your body language supports and projects your verbal language. Sit up straight in your chair; do not slump. Maintain simple and natural good posture in a relaxed, attentive manner throughout the interview.

EYE CONTACT. Maintain proper eye contact throughout the interview. A person who fails to look the interviewer in the eye *appears* to be untrustworthy, untruthful, and hypocritical. By no means should you conduct a staring contest, however. No matter who wins that kind of tussle, you *lose*.

PROJECT ASSURANCE. Try not to fidget or jiggle your extremities. Any sign of such a tic hints at basic nervousness—and a basic nervousness is a tip-off to inner insecurity, fear, or lack of self-esteem. In the argot of the sixties: *Be cool, my man*.

EXHIBIT CONFIDENCE. Make the proper movements with your body to underline a key point. Do not overgesticulate—too much hand-waving and eye-popping can distract your interviewer from the very point you are trying to engrave on his mind.

BE POLITE. Smile from time to time, nod, and establish a good personal rapport with the interviewer throughout the exchange. Always be friendly, warm, and polite. Do not oversmile or the grin will seem to be frozen on with plaster of paris.

SHOW SENSITIVITY. Do not try to dominate the discussion, or you will put the interviewer on the defensive. By being dominated, the interviewer will become upset and may turn hostile. What you strive for is a two-way, open-ended, balanced conversation.

REMAIN POSITIVE. Do not volunteer any negative information to the interviewer. If negatives do surface, be honest about them, but be brief! Never overexplain an embarrassing episode. Actually, it is best if you follow the old-fashioned rule of thumb known by all servicemen the world over: *"Never explain." "Never apologize."*

READING THE PROSPECT = READING THE EMPLOYER

In getting to the heart of the prospect, you seek out emotions to stimulate the following: pride, fear, envy, and so on. In getting to the heart of the prospective employer, you seek to discover as quickly as you can the various emotional issues that are the key to the interviewer's hiring decisions.

Since you must work swiftly in this rather difficult area, watch carefully as your interviewer speaks or as he or she reacts to your speech. If there is a sign of unusual interest or excitement, identify the reason as quickly as you can. Then spend a bit of time to exploit this interest and satisfy your interviewer's curiosity.

Likewise, watch carefully for evidence of your interviewer's interest or lack of interest in specific ideas that you have already researched about him or about the company for which he works. In this way you can discover exactly what kind of candidate the job calls for. And you can frame yourself as the ideal person to hold the job.

In dealing with a job interviewer, you must not be as manipulative as you would be if you were dealing with a sales prospect. Nevertheless, the very same psychological determinants operate in the job interviewer as in the product prospect. It is up to you to stimulate the proper emotional response, and then operate on it in such a way that you can prove you can handle a certain aspect of the job—with determination, with confidence, and with certainty of improvement.

WHEN TO CLOSE = WHEN TO DECIDE

The ability to *read* your interviewer will give you a proper sense of the time to make your decision. It's a truism: You have been interviewing the employer and he or she has been interviewing you as well. You now come to a point in the middle game when you make up your mind either to try to go ahead or to back out.

You can determine a great deal by a simple study of the interviewer's body language—in the same way he or she is studying you. Thus you can at any time by a glance decide how the conversation is going with the interviewer:

> A SMILE. A smile tells you that you are definitely on the right track.
>
> A NOD. A nod of the head in an affirmative manner tells you that your interviewer agrees with what you are saying.
>
> A FROWN. A frown tells you that you have lost his or her interest and should renew that interest quickly or head for the door.
>
> A SCOWL. A scowl tells you that your interviewer disagrees with what you are saying and in addition rejects you as a possible candidate.
>
> BODILY RESTLESSNESS. A degree of bodily restlessness on the part of the interviewer is a warning to you to change your direction or your intent.

Of course, you can fight back even if your interviewer has been turned off by you; it all depends on how much you want the job. If you do fight back, try to do it in a telling fashion. Remember, if you win—fine. If you lose—there are other jobs.

My point is that a wimp never wins. You must be decisive—even if it gets your head chopped off.

A DIGRESSION IN DEPTH

I'd like to break in here with some trenchant thoughts about the job situation at the present time. It has a great deal to do with how to handle the job interview these days.

What Industry Wants from You

Time was, employers simply hired warm bodies to help out around the work area. After World War II, for example, prosperity was so much in evidence in America that anyone who could show up in the morning and last out to the evening could hold any kind of job.

In the past few years a tremendous change has occurred. The country is still prosperous, yes. But a glance at the financial pages of the newspapers will show that powerful forces—both economic and social—are at work and beginning to revolutionize employment selection and the interview process.

The warm body concept is out. O.U.T. For the moment let's take a sideways glance at what *is* happening "out there."

Who Won the War, Anyway?

The two countries the United States was fighting in World War II are now back on their feet financially—thanks mostly to the largesse and liberality of the United States of America, or "Uncle Sam," as the *Daily News* in New York used to call it editorially. These two countries are now running the U.S. ragged in industrial competition.

The reason is simple. Foreign manufacturers can use

cheap labor and cheap materials to beat us out. Generally speaking, a foreign manufacturer can turn out a product comparable to our best for a great deal less money; sometimes the product is far superior to our own!

West Germany and Japan (our old enemies) now hold a decided competitive advantage in the marketplace worldwide. Our own foreign trade deficit acts as a barometer of the seriousness of the problem.

Two Basic Concepts

U.S. labor is not getting too much money; it simply demands an amount far in excess of foreign labor. Yet with the competition so fierce, American companies are focusing on every facet of their operations to bring about improvement in their productivity, their quality, and their costs.

And so—

Two new concepts are overshadowing everything else in management's perception of employment. These two concepts are:

- How to reduce costs
- How to increase employee productivity

Write out these two concepts on paper and mount it near the mirror into which you peer every morning. Let them be engraved on your mind. Never lose sight of those two basic ideas. They can win you a job. Without them, you are lost.

That Special "Value Added" Concept in Hiring

Concentrating on these two concepts has caused a dramatic change in hiring policies. No longer does a company take on an employee to fill the spot vacated by the last-to-leave warm body. The company hires an employee to fill the spot, and to add a degree of increased productivity to the job at the same time!

Thus the aggressive newcomer who knows how to produce more work in the time on the job becomes the candidate who wins out—not the more genteel protean man in the gray flannel suit of a much earlier and more naive era.

There is then a "value added" concept to the current modus operandi of hiring. What I'm saying is that you can use your sales techniques to much greater advantage today in seeking a new job than you could formerly.

> TIME WAS: Mangement didn't want anyone on board who rocked the boat.
>
> TIME IS: Management wants somebody to rock the boat and sink it if need be. Sink it and build another to replace it.

The Day of the Movers and Shakers

You must focus on a far wider strategy than formerly to get the job you want. You must think more about what you can do for the company you're trying to work for rather than just make yourself fit into the groove that is already there.

It's the movers and shakers who are getting ahead.

You must be a mover and shaker today—not just a sitter and rooster.

Now, with this aside completed, let's go back to our discussion of the job interview where we left it—at the moment of decision. At the moment you decide to go for the job or not to go for it.

Make up Your Mind

Now is the time in the interview to decide to go on and tell your interviewer that you'd like to be considered, or to decide to back out of the project and make your graceful but determined exit.

This is usually at the point the interviewer will put it to you in firm, clear, certain terms:

INTERVIEWER: And exactly how do you feel you can help our company in its day-to-day operation?

Actually, the terms may not be so clear or so firm—but this point always arrives and it is the crucial point at which you should begin your Countdown from Five.

THE JOB INTERVIEW: COUNTDOWN FROM FIVE

This is the moment you've been waiting for. This is the moment you've made all your preparations beforehand for. This is the moment you can make it or break it. It is a vantage point, the top of the mountain, so to speak.

It is the spot where you can shine—or flicker out.

Frankly, it all depends on how well you've done your homework. The homework I refer to is the amount of research, study, and thinking you have put into your preliminary data gathering about the company and the people in it.

Profile of the Job

Let's do a bit of analyzing here. In researching the position you are being interviewed for, you have been able to put together a fairly comprehensive picture of what is required of the job holder. That is, you have at least been able to find out more than what was mentioned in the short newspaper ad description.

Or, perhaps, you have been able to put together a much more detailed profile.

Whatever you have done, make sure that you study it carefully, commit it to memory, and carry it with you at all times.

Do you have all that down?

Good. Now take your job profile and tear up the paper it is written on and burn it.

That's right:

Destroy it!

It's not worth a snowflake in hell.

The Real Job Profile Faces Ahead!

Harken back to my digression in the middle of this chapter. Think of the two concepts I was talking about:

Reduce costs.
Raise productivity.

Think about each of them in relation to the job profile that is in your memory bank.

The trick is to see how you can turn the "job that was" into the "job that will be"—the job that will *reduce costs* and *raise productivity*.

That's the job profile you must fashion for yourself. That is the job profile that you should have well in mind when you are fed that open-ended question by your interviewer.

The procedure to follow is immediately to ask the interviewer a question somewhat like this:

"I am interested in your organization's short- and long-term strategic objectives. And I would like to be in a position to do something about them."

Long-Range Planning and the Future

Once you find out what the company has in mind, *then* you can look into your own mind to see which of these broad concepts you can use to elucidate your profile of the "job that will be."

With that you can position yourself as an employee and

you can suggest positive changes that can be effectuated to help the organization reach its future goals. Although the interview at this moment becomes more or less a think piece about the future, it will give your interviewer a good idea of where your thoughts are coming from.

In fact, it puts you and your interviewer on a common level, without the obligatory props of the interview hovering over the conversation.

A Good Rule of Thumb

Do not stop here. Add to your portrayal of the future a number of concrete changes you might make. By now you have not only made it clear that you have thought a great deal about the job you are applying for, but you have considered the company and the people in it as well.

All this is a plus for you in the eyes of the interviewer.

You have shown him or her that not only do you fit the job description to a T, but you also have enough imagination and savvy to mold the job into something far better than it is, and far more productive than it is.

You clinch the idea that you are the person for the job.

And you get it!

10

The Business Deal: Countdown from Five

Doing business is dull? Who says so?

"I'm always looking for more excitement in life," one man recently said—a man who spends most of his time putting business deals together. "It's *doing* something," he said, "that makes life exciting. It's achieving something. It's the thrill of doing."

He went on to say: "And part of the reason it's exciting is because they are megadeals. They are important deals. They are glamorous deals. Everybody talks about them. Everybody reads about them and writes about them. There's a level of importance there that, I think, also turns me on."

Donald Trump speaking.

This man, who called his autobiography *The Art of the Deal*, should know whereof he speaks. He is today the biggest maker of deals in this country.

MILLIONS AND MILLIONS AND MILLIONS

"In actuality," he once said, "thousands and thousands of people are put to work" when he makes a deal. "Millions and hundreds of millions of dollars in taxes are paid."

That's the difference between a *business* deal and a simple sales transaction or a simple job interview.

Even in the world of Donald Trump and other movers and shakers, the last five minutes of the deal are absolutely the most crucial moments of the entire affair. It is the point in time when all the i's are dotted and the t's crossed.

Let's look at the elements that go to make those last five minutes in a typical business deal so important—as opposed to a regular sales closing or a job interview.

We'll take a leaf out of Donald Trump's book for a bird's-eye view of such a negotiated agreement—a very complicated one involving megabucks—to illustrate the importance of *preparing* ahead of time for those last five minutes. To quote a fictional character, John "Hannibal" Smith, leader of the famous television "A Team": "I love it when a good plan comes together."

It is the coming together in those last five minutes that puts paid to all the work that has gone into arranging the various elements for that final coming together, that fusion of complicated and conflicting complexities into a completed unit.

THE REJUVENATION OF FORTY-SECOND STREET

Donald Trump took his first plunge into Manhattan construction when he decided to purchase the rundown Commodore Hotel from the bankrupt Penn Central Railroad, which owned it, to remodel it. At first he planned to do a simple refurbishing job.

He had no money to buy the hotel with. Investigation showed Trump that the Commodore was dying; it owed New York City $6 million in back taxes. Trump struck a deal with

Victor Palmieri, who acted for Penn Central, to allow Trump to have an exclusive option to buy the Commodore Hotel for the sum of $250,000.

Trump then persuaded an architect named Der Scutt to draw up plans for a *new* hotel to take the place of the Commodore; he felt that by building a brand-new hotel, he might be able to attract a partner who would put up the construction money for him.

For One Dollar . . .

The plans for the new hotel appealed to the Hyatt Hotel chain, which agreed to finance the construction for equal partnership in the new hotel. Trump and Hyatt together would buy the Commodore from Penn Central for $10 million, $6 million of which would go to the City of New York for back taxes.

Trump then used the lure of the $6 million in back taxes to persuade the City of New York to give him a tax abatement over a period of forty years. The city would not agree and the deal almost fell through.

Then Trump worked out a scheme in which he and Hyatt would sell the hotel for one dollar to New York State's Urban Development Corporation, which would lease it back to Trump for ninety-nine years. Trump's rent, in lieu of property taxes, would start at $250,000 a year, and rise in the fortieth year to $2.7 million. And Trump would pay the City of New York a percentage of the profits.

At that point, no money had yet changed hands. All the elements of the deal were hanging fire, as it were. However, Trump soon persuaded Equitable Life Assurance Society and the Bronx Savings Bank to finance the deal.

Trump and the Hyatt chain then announced the deal to the public. It caused a sensation. No money had yet changed hands. The deal was all based on word of mouth and trust. When Trump was asked later why the City of New York was willing to give him a forty-year tax abatement—when no one else could get one—he replied: "Because I didn't ask for fifty."

Note carefully the complicated arrangements that Trump had to make in order to get this deal to fly. In point of fact, because of the deal, the glitzy and extremely successful Grand Hyatt Hotel rose from the ashes of the Commodore. Donald Trump was launched on a career that from that moment has escalated into a Horatio Alger story without parallel.

How Did He Work It?

It's interesting to note how every element in the house of cards Trump was erecting was linked to another in a backward chain of effect and cause.

Thus:

1. In effect, the tax abatement deal depended on whether or not Trump and the Hyatt chain could get financing for the construction of the new hotel.

2. Financing depended on the credibility of Trump and his associates actually to be able to construct the new hotel.

3. The Hyatt chain's agreement to become Trump's partner by putting up the construction money depended on Trump's ability to produce viable plans for the new hotel.

4. Trump's ability to pay for the option to purchase the Commodore depended on his ability to convince people he could pull off the arrangements he had conceived.

5. Even Der Scutt's drawing of the plans was dependent on his belief in Trump's ability to pay him for the job.

Look to the Last Five Minutes

Thus Donald Trump's success with the Grand Hyatt illustrates a number of important points in the art of closing a complex business deal—that is, with every move made, to concentrate *always* on the last five minutes when the final deal will be cut and all the pieces fall into place.

Let's look at each of these important points one by one, referring at random to the Trump deal, in order to illustrate the technique of working out complex business arrangements that have to be right, detail by detail, to lead to the proper consummation in those crucial last five minutes.

KNOW YOUR GOALS IN DETAIL

First and foremost, any good businessperson involved in making a complex deal with someone else or some other company, must always know exactly what he or she wants before even *beginning* to structure a deal.

You must know in detail just what you want at the very outset. Although perhaps Donald Trump did not know that he was going to produce the Grand Hyatt Hotel when he started, he did know that he wanted to improve the shambles that had been the Commodore Hotel. He knew that the city should want a better hotel there—that was the reason he came up with his tax abatement deal.

In devising a business deal with another businessperson, you should begin talking only after you are sure as to the exact goal you seek to achieve, the exact amount of money you want to spend or receive, the number of players who will be in the closing of the deal, the deadline for the final signing of the contracts, and the budget that must be set aside for working out the arrangements.

Without these details in mind, you may self-destruct before you get to the closing.

THE IMPORTANCE OF BEING FLEXIBLE

There is a great deal to be said for always preparing at least two ways of doing anything you set out to do, which might be called Plan A and Plan B. Plan B is of course the fallback plan—what to do if Plan A is found to be unworkable.

It is wise always to have a good escape route planned for

failures that might develop during the first moves you make. You can then rest at a fallback position and plan a new attack.

In Donald Trump's elaborate scheme to rejuvenate Forty-second Street, he was always flexible; he could always alter his plans in small details and in large ones. When he was putting together the complicated details of his moves, he had elaborate fallback positions available: Plans A, B, C, D, and E—probably many more.

Your own business proposal will be a great deal less complicated than Donald Trump's was. However, you should study his techniques and realize that for every plan you make, there should be three or four different strategies that you can follow immediately, if your original one falters.

Remember that the best-laid schemes have a way of going sour, through no fault of the individuals who dream them up. Oftentimes, a third or fourth plan may prove to be the most feasible one of all, and the one that actually brings you to your sought-after goal.

Be flexible, be ingenious, be quick in seeking out and finding another way to go.

SHARE THE CREDIT

One of the most annoying and pervasive habits of the human being is to reach out and gather unto himself or herself the credit for a marvelous thing that *you* accomplished, instigated, or developed.

In the corporate structure as you work your way slowly up the slippery rungs of the ladder, you have actually been robbed of credit for a successful idea any number of times. And credit is the way you achieve stature and elevation in the corporate hive.

During the process of negotiating a deal, however, you must quell your instincts to grab for credit. The same is true in a way with a salesperson who forces credit for an idea on a prospective customer.

One of the best ways to get another person to agree to a

line of action in a negotiation is to persuade him or her that your idea is his or hers. And to do this, you must forget your own instinctive negative reactions to sharing credit.

Note in particular how Donald Trump turned this particular ploy to his advantage throughout his dealings in the Grand Hyatt project. His first thought must have been to garner all the credit for his idea of building a new hotel. However, when it came down to the nitty-gritty, he not only shared the hotel itself after it was built with the Grand Hyatt chain—in partnership! (the absolute negation of total credit)—but he also shared the ownership of the hotel property with the City of New York, since he now only *leases* the property.

He made his idea *their* idea by letting them share in the credit of the project he was putting together. And it worked!

WHAT'S IN IT FOR ME?

It is a proven fact that you cannot get something for nothing. That is, every product has its price; every service costs money; every exchange that is made with money as the medium of exchange costs *something*. No one gets a big deal for nothing. You always get just what you pay for.

You must constantly remind the businessperson you are dealing with that indeed he or she is not doing something for you for nothing, that there is strictly a decent advantage in doing business with you.

That is, you must never forget to stress continually exactly what the other person is getting out of the deal you are trying to arrange. If you fail to do so, you will find your opposite number losing interest and beginning to stare out the window at the passing clouds.

Note how Trump was able to give something to every one he dealt with.

- He gave $10 million to the Penn Central for the old Commodore Hotel.
- He gave the City of New York $6 million of that $10 million.

- He actually paid Penn Central $4 million, after the $6 million was deducted.
- He gave the Hyatt chain a half interest in the finished hotel.
- He gave the Grand Hyatt Hotel to the city in return for a ninety-nine-year lease.

Trump himself, of course, got a little something from everybody. From the city, he got a very generous tax abatement. From the Hyatt chain he got construction money. From Equitable and Bronx Savings he got the money to finance the deal.

What's in it for me?

Plenty!

Make sure it sounds good—and at the same time make sure it's the truth!

GET A "YES" EARLY ON

Back in Chapter 4, "The Art of Conversation Control," I pointed out how you could control a conversation by the interrogative technique, that is, you could steer a discussion any way you wanted to by asking the proper *questions.*

In negotiations, the same rule applies. But in addition to the matter of controlling the conversation, there is a psychological fillip to breaking the ice with your opposite number early in the game.

The way to do it is to force the conversation into a pattern in which you can elicit a nod and a definite "yes" from your opposite number. From the moment that magic nod occurs and that "yes" sounds out, you're a long step nearer to complete rapport with your opposite number.

It may sound dumb, but it certainly does pay off in the long run. Believe me. I'm not sure I understand the psychology of it, if there is any, but I know it always works. For example, there is usually a point at which the conversation lulls, at which things slow down, at which the end seems near—and you lean back, smile, and say:

"There are a number of points we *do* agree on, aren't there?"

The obvious answer is the only one that can possibly follow. "Yes."

"Then let's go over them one by one!"

A nod.

It's *that* easy!

GET A "NO" EARLY ON

The above rule has a corollary. You guessed it: it has to do with forcing your opposite number to say "no" to something.

The obvious way to do it is to state a figure for some part of the project you are working on that is so ridiculous that the thought of it is enough to blow anyone's mind.

"No!"

That's all you need.

By having elicited this "no" you're another giant step forward toward reaching a final agreement on your whole proposal.

Again, I have no idea why this is so—I simply know that it is.

TAKE ADVANTAGE OF THE ADVANTAGES

Another solid rule for you to remember during any business negotiations leading up to a closing is to continue to have at least one benefit or advantage at hand to balance out any objection or disadvantage pointed out by your opposite number. When there are no objections on the floor for discussion, it is a good time to talk about all the advantages you are providing the other party.

Of course, this lesson about pointing out advantages to outweigh disadvantages is old hat for most salespersons, but it never hurts to continue reminding people of it. You'd be surprised how many people forget to keep plugging the good things on their side.

As has been noted before in this book, you don't always have to come up with a parallel advantage for every disadvantage. The idea is for you to mark your advantages well in your mind so you can bring them up for instant discussion during a barrage of disadvantages from the person you are negotiating with.

The idea is to answer every objection with a benefit.

Advantages are not always easy to come by; disadvantages seem to proliferate. The point in the above discussion is a simple one. Improve your strengths, not your weaknesses. You are not in business to educate yourself; you are in business to win the best terms you can.

Bury the weaknesses you know of. In baseball, the axiom is well known. *Go to your strength.* If you're a great batter, don't practice catching; practice batting. If you're a great fielder, don't worry too much about hitting; practice fielding.

Play to your advantages, and try not to focus too much on your disadvantages. If you make the most of your advantages, your disadvantages will take care of themselves.

‖ I WONDER WHAT WOULD HAPPEN IF . . .

I was always curious about what prompted that weird adjustment in the Trump deal in which the builders of the Grand Hyatt Hotel were required to sell the finished structure for one dollar to the Urban Development Corporation, which would then lease it back to the owners for ninety-nine years. But it occurs to me that it was an ingenious way of overcoming a basic objection; that objection must have been the city's reluctance to let Trump own the land and the hotel forever.

In fact, I remember thinking once that probably Trump leaned back in his chair when he was on a collision course with the city fathers and sighed:

"I wonder what would happen if I didn't own the hotel and the land at all, and simply leased it from the City of New York?"

Floating the Trial Balloon

If that was the way it happened, Trump was doing what every businessperson has done more than once in a critical situation. He simply unloosed a trial balloon and watched it float into the air. Had he come right out with the proposition—"Look. I'll build the hotel and give it to you. You lease it back to me for ninety-nine years."—it is likely the city fathers would have shaken their heads, no.

Whether or not that trial balloon was ever launched or not makes no difference. The point is, it's a marvelous way of getting an idea out into the open where it can be studied objectively. A trial balloon *belongs* to no one. It floats in the air. If the opposition picks up on it, then it becomes the opposition's idea. It's a good way to share the ideas to balance out the pros and cons.

When you're hung up sometime on a sticky point of business, remember to lean back, close your eyes, and murmur distantly:

"I wonder what would happen if. . . ."

KEEP SOMETHING TO GIVE BACK

For a poker player, it's always good to have an ace in the hole.

For a businessperson, it's always good to have an ace in the hole, too.

It's easier for a businessperson to procure an ace in the hole than it is for a card player, who must wait for the disposition of the cards for the favor.

The ace in the hole for the businessperson becomes something you hold back for use later on as a bargaining tool. In effect, you should always try to keep just a little something back so you can bargain with it later. Sometimes that "something" may simply be your original request for *more* than you really want up front. When the going gets rough, you can always ease back a little—give up that ace you've been holding—and get an agreement.

Thus your opposite number thinks he or she has won the point.

You know yourself that you have won the point hands down.

A corollary to asking for more than you want is never to let your opposite number have as much as he or she wants.

Because you have made deals before, you know that he or she will be dealing exactly the way you are dealing. Just be firm and never let yourself be worn down.

GET IT ALL DOWN IN WRITING

The closer you come to closing, the closer you come to paperwork. And paperwork means getting down all the details of the long discussions you have had into writing.

Up to now in this chapter I've been talking about preliminaries to closing—the moves that lead up to the last five minutes. Those last five minutes are the minutes in which you finally lean forward, take a pen in your hand, and sign the contract that has been drawn up through your long processes of negotiating.

Now those last five minutes are here. Now you have to settle down and make sure that all the details are correct, that all the i's are dotted and all the t's are crossed.

> *One last point:* In any final negotiations, you must have an attorney to represent you, especially when it comes to signing on the dotted line. I'm sure your opposite number will have representation. There are attorneys who make a business of knowing about contract law.

Getting down to the contract is getting down to the last five minutes of business. If you have any questions, make sure you voice them out loud. Make sure too that you are firm with your opposite number. Do not let the conversation move on until you have had a satisfactory answer—or a satisfactory emendation in the contract.

Once you and your opposite number are satisfied with the contract as it stands, the two of you must sign it and at that moment the deal is a fait accompli.

For better or for worse.

For richer or for poorer.

SHOW YOUR GRATITUDE

It's all over. The contracts are signed. You shake hands with your opposite number. Everyone is all smiles. The lawyers have earned big fees. You and your opposite number have made a good deal. Everyone is happy.

The next day sit down and write a note of gratitude to your opposite number. Write it sincerely, thanking him or her for the courtesy extended to you, for the consideration given you, for all the good things that have come out of the long round of negotiations.

Silly?

Excessively pandering?

No! It never hurts to pat someone on the back after a deal is made.

It's better than disappearing quickly into the dark and raising a question in other people's minds about the hastiness of your departure.

HOW TO HANDLE A COMPLEX BUSINESS DEAL

The success or failure of a business deal depends to a large extent on your *attitude* when you go into discussion—your attitude and the attitude of your opposite number.

For the book, here are five important elements in your attitude that may decide the outcome of difficult negotiations. You should always consider them before you sit down to hash out your differences:

- Commitment
- Honesty
- Enthusiasm
- Eloquence
- Humor

If you can somehow think of these five musts and consider the importance they will cast on your discussions, you will be able to project them to your opposite number.

As you can see, each is an important part of the attitude that you project as you face your opposite number.

Do's and Don'ts for Negotiations

Here is a guideline for you to follow in sitting down to work out a business deal with someone else. It is in the form of two lists: do's for the negotiator; and don'ts for the negotiator.

Let's put the "don'ts" first:

Do Not

1. Never turn a negotiation into a confrontation. This is a *discussion*, not a *battle*.
2. No matter how hard you push, be sure you *never* compromise on principles.
3. Do not try to represent yourself—always have an attorney to represent you. "He who represents himself has a fool for a client."
4. Never, never, never get mad! You will lose every advantage you thought you had won.
5. Don't come down too fast when your opposite number refuses a figure you have in mind. Slowly, slowly.
6. Never meet in the opposition's office. Choose neutral ground—preferably your attorney's office.

Do

1. Repeat this motto and paste it on the mirror just below where your face appears: "Nice guys finish first."
2. Play fair, work hard, be gracious, always deal in good faith—and you'll *win*.
3. Decency is *not* a weakness. Be tough, be hard, be efficient, but above all, be *nice*.
4. Create an atmosphere of calmness and repose. Be forthright and positive. But be able to compromise.
5. Always qualify the person you are dealing with. Qualify the company. Do your homework!
6. Force the other side to be the first to come up with a definite offer.

11

How to Close with a Smile

Getting back to the original concept of this book, any kind of one-on-one interview—a sales discussion, a job interview, a business deal—eventually follows the general lines of a game of chess, in exactly the way I described at the beginning of the book.

For example:

- THE OPENING GAMBIT involves a kind of probing on both sides.
- THE MIDDLE GAME involves persuasion and objection—the give-and-take of any kind of interview, confrontation, or type of verbal intercourse.
- THE END GAME is the crux of the matter: it is the moment when all the issues become resolved and the sale is either made—or killed.

THE PROPER EXIT LINE

I'd like to say more right now about the proper method of concluding any interview, meeting, or confrontation.

IN A SALES INTERVIEW, the sale is consummated by the signing of the contract.

IN A JOB INTERVIEW, the final move is either the hiring or the nonhiring of the individual seeking the job.

IN A BUSINESS DEAL, the closing moves constitute an agreement between two contenders, or the lack of such an agreement.

As you can see, the possibilities dwindle down to a precious two:

• Successful consummation of sale
• Lack of consummation of sale

Now let's look at the proper way for you to handle either one of these two eventualities. The manner in which you handle them is a key to your future dealings with your prospect, your potential employer, or your antagonist and (possibly) future associate in a business situation.

How to Win without Showing It

You've got the prospect's signature on the dotted line. (Actually, most lines for signatures are not dotted at all these days, but are simple printed underlines over which the signator affixes his or her name. So much for clichés.)

The truth of the matter is—you've won!

You want to jump up and down and shout with glee. You've just made a commission of five thousand bucks. Wow! It's time to fly to the moon and back. It's champagne for all.

It's jump up and down and wave your arms in the air like a fullback who's just run the ball over the goal line.

What do you *really* do? I mean, what are you *supposed* to do?

Here it is. Read it and weep:

You sit calmly back and you smile gently. Nothing that happens on this earth is going to upset your equilibrium. It's all in a day's work. What if you have spent nine months getting this thing to fly? Well, so what? After all, mothers spend nine months getting children ready to be born, don't they? Everything's relative.

You play it this way:

You're considerate of your prospect, because you have been able to help him or her make a right decision. After all, the prospect is going to be the one who should be cheering— not you. You have simply helped out at a crucial time— assisted in the midwiving of the product or service that is going to make your customer's life a happy one.

Step by step: You congratulate the prospect, pointing out that certainly he or she did the *right* thing. You bring it down to a personal level, if you wish; that's one way of continuing the rapport you have established throughout the sales pitch.

> "My uncle purchased a Ford Escort last month, the same way you have done. Let me tell you, he's the happiest man in the family. He's getting better mileage out of it—and he's happy with the way it *rides*. You should feel proud that you've made the kind of decision you have."

That brings the thing into the proper personalized setting, and establishes a good level of friendship between seller and buyer. You haven't plundered him or her—you've *helped* in a tough time of decision-making.

As your buyer walks out, you shake hands and smile naturally, holding back any excess of glee, which would be misread as a gloating look on the face of someone who's just done in someone else. *That* is a "no-no."

There are at least two reasons for this kind of attitude:

- A safety net
- A future sale

Let's explore the safety-net aspect for the moment.

The Safety-Net Aspect. Suppose the pleasure boat you've just sold a prospect develops a bad leak within a month. It's not the fault of the manufacturer. Nobody knows whose fault it is.

The buyer comes to you huffing and puffing and breathing smoke out of his nostrils. What to do?

Because you've established the proper rapport with him or her during those crucial closing moments of the sale, you can reassure him or her that all will be well, and contact the company that made the boat. Your prospect believes you and you are thus able to help handle a sticky situation in a fashion that will satisfy everybody in the end.

In a case like this, you do not simply ignore the buyer, but you do everything you can to help get the situation ironed out in a reasonable fashion. If you have acted in a straightforward manner throughout your dealings with him or her, even if solving the crisis costs the buyer money, he or she will not resent *you.* You have done everything right. You have acted as a backup in a time of need. And so on.

Now, let's explore the future-sale aspect.

The Future-Sale Aspect. The answering device you've sold a prospect works fine—so well, in fact, that the prospect wants a bigger model.

Now, if you've treated this buyer as an idiot you've put something over on, he or she is not going to come back to you to get a bigger model. He or she is going somewhere else!

The fact that you have treated your prospect with every consideration throughout your dealings with him or her means that there is a good chance of another sale sometime in the future.

By treating this as a helping-out exercise, you have made your prospect happy in the knowledge that you are there to serve him or her, not to do a fleecing job.

Even if it does not seem as if there will be a future sale, do not at any point cause your prospect to think that you've put one over on him or her. Even if you *have.*

How to Lose Without Showing It

Winning is one thing. The adrenaline works and the personality expands and the psyche is refurbished. Everything is
right with the world. But losing is not so easy. Losing is a
great trauma to the psyche. Losing ruins the persona. It puts
gray in your hair. It pulls the corners of your mouth down.

If the sale falls through, what to do?

Here's what you *do:*

You have to put on an act. It is not easy. But the moves
are all there, presorted for you, and organized to show your
aplomb, your sangfroid that you are not cowed by his or her
rejection. You do not take the loss personally at all. You tell
yourself that, in the words of the Godfather's soldiers:
"Nothing personal. It's business, you know."

It *is* personal, damn it! It is horrendously, murderously,
killingly personal, and your ego lies in shreds at your feet.
You are disconsolate. You want to weep. But—no tears. No
frowns. No grief.

You straighten up, smile naturally, speak charmingly to
your prospect as he or she strides out into the sunshine.
You've lost, but you look like the winner that you are. Inside?
Underneath? Whatever.

These are your moves! MAKE THEM!

- Play it cool.
- Play it likable.
- Play it like a *winner.*
- Wait till next time!

The Anger That Comes . . .

Above all, never—repeat, *never!*—allow yourself to become
the victim of anger.

I must say this because there is a cliché in the psychological counseling racket that says something to the effect that

"anger is a good thing for you." The theory behind this dubious concept is that by expressing your anger, and letting it work on you, you are able to let out your inner feelings, and because your inner feelings are freed from your psyche and not bottled up there, you are a better and more relaxed person.

The aftermath to this action is that since you and your respondent have aired your differences and exposed your true feelings to one another, the atmosphere around you is cleared and whatever grievances you had no longer exist.

Forget it!

I look on anger as a destructive force, quite rightly designated as one of humankind's most hidden and dangerous all-time motivators. I think the people who invented the Seven Deadly Sins were *right* to include anger.

It is not only self-destructive, but it can destroy others as well. It can turn back on itself and destroy everything that has been built up between two people, ruining a potential relationship forever.

I do not believe that anger is a fine safety valve. I do not urge you to blow your top whenever you feel like it. Instead I warn you never to succumb to anger in your dealings with another person. Swallow it. Perhaps it will fester for a while. In the long run, you'll be better off not letting yourself come under its dubious and sometimes frightening sway.

- Anger breeds resentment.
- Anger breeds more anger.
- Anger breeds ruin.
- Anger leaves bitterness in its wake.

Never let anger turn against you. Self-hate is a negative emotion. Never let anger turn outward onto others. It is dangerous to any kind of bridge you are trying to build to others.

Fire your psychologist.

Swallow your rancor. It can only hurt to let the beast out of its cage.

(Suggested Rereading: Chapter 5. Just in case you're not the one to let loose the anger, but are its recipient. There are ways of handling it on the receiving end.)

Keep Those Lines of Communication Open!

In any business relationship, it is a rule of thumb always to keep the lines of communication—any lines of communication—wide open. Communication itself is a two-way street, not a one-way road to your own selfish ends. The only contact between business associates *is* communication. To close it down or to allow it to be cluttered with DETOUR, TAKE NEXT EXIT, or DO NOT PROCEED signs is to shut down all means of communication.

It's time to run through a review of the basic elements of communication.

The Nature of Communication

Communication involves the transmission and reception of data. Good communication involves the movement of an idea, a datum, an impression, a message, or a feeling from one person to another with only minimal distortion of meaning in the process.

The ideal is to convey data from the sender to the receiver without any distortion at all.

Confirmation of the transmission is sometimes overlooked in a brief analysis of communication. However, without some kind of confirmation that A's idea has been sent to and received by B, there is no solid indication that any communication per se has been achieved.

Thus this confirmation is an essential part of the transaction. It is proper confirmation that is involved most heavily in the final five minutes of any business transaction, whether it be a sales interview, a job interview, or any kind of business interview.

Both sides must absolutely understand one another in the closing moment of any interview. The persuader must understand exactly what he or she is trying to tell the persuadee; the persuadee must understand clearly what he or she is getting in the product or service that is under consideration and how much is going to be paid for it.

Both sides must understand clearly all the details of the transaction that is being firmed up. Both sides must be on exactly the same wavelength in order to make the confirmation truly an agreement in toto—an agreement that is completely comprehended by both sides and has been agreed to honestly and sincerely.

ATTITUDE, CONFIRMATION, AND EXIT LINES

As much as you must manifest the proper attitude and demeanor in your persona, you as the persuader, seller, or job seeker must take it upon yourself to make sure that the transaction is completely *understood* by your persuadee. Otherwise the transaction is not a proper fait accompli, even if it has been technically completed by the signing of a paper.

I simply cannot stress too vehemently the need for absolute clarity on both sides—understanding of all the myriad details and elements of the contract that is signed at the windup of any business transaction.

Thus, any proper confirmation *includes* an understanding of the tiny print in any document relating to the business transaction, as well as the simple facts and figures on an ordinary order pad used for a less complex business deal.

Remember this: SALESMANSHIP *IS* COMMUNICATION.

And the clincher: GOOD SALESMANSHIP IS COMMUNICATION *CONFIRMED!*

INDEX

ABOUT THE AUTHOR

Multimillionaire Norman King lectures widely and is the author of ten major books, including *The Money Messiahs*, a Book-of-the-Month Fortune selection. Acknowledged by *Advertising Age* as the dean of barter and capital recovery, he is today a renowned international merchant banker, one of the few with constant access to bank financial instruments used as collateral and for investment.

He resides with his wife, Barbara, and French poodle, Sugar, in New York City.